James Patterson

by

James Patterson

The Stories of My Life

LITTLE, BROWN AND COMPANY

LARGE PRINT EDITION

Little, Brown and Company
Hachette Book Group
1290 Avenue of the Americas, New York, NY 10104
First edition: June 2022

Little, Brown and Company is a division of Hachette Book Group, Inc. The Little, Brown name and logo are trademarks of Hachette Book Group, Inc.

The publisher is not responsible for websites (or their content) that are not owned by the publisher.

The Hachette Speakers Bureau provides a wide range of authors for speaking events. To find out more, go to hachettespeakersbureau.com or call (866) 376-6591.

Book design by Marie Mundaca

ISBN 9780316397537 (hardcover) / 9780316445214 (large print) / 9780316490757 (signed edition) / 9780316490641 (B&N signed edition)
LCCN 2021943106

Printing 1, 2022

LSC-C

Printed in the United States of America

James Patterson

by

James Patterson

i want to tell you some
stories
…the way i remember
them anyway.

hungry dogs run faster

THIS MORNING, I got up at quarter to six. Late for me. I made strong coffee and oatmeal with a sprinkle of brown sugar and a touch of cream. I leafed through the *New York Times, USA Today,* and the *Wall Street Journal.* Then I took a deep breath and started this ego-biography that you're reading.

My grandmother once told me, "You're lucky if you find something in life you like to do. Then it's a miracle if somebody'll pay you to do it." Well, I'm living a miracle. I spend my days, and many nights, writing stories about Alex Cross, the Women's Murder Club, Maximum Ride, the Kennedys, John Lennon, young Muhammad Ali, and now *this.*

My writing style is colloquial, which is the way we talk to one another, right? Some might disagree—some vehemently disagree—but I think colloquial storytelling is a valid form of expression. If you wrote down your favorite story to tell, there might not be any great sentences, but it still could be outstanding. Try it out. Write down a good story you tell friends—maybe starting with the line "Stop me if I've told you this one before"—and see how it looks on paper.

A word about my office. Come in. Look around. A well-worn, hopelessly cluttered writing table sits at the center, surrounded by shelves filled to the brim with my favorite books, which I dip into all the time.

At the base of the bookshelves are counters. Today, there are thirty-one of my manuscripts on these surfaces. Every time journalists come to my office and see the thirty or so manuscripts in progress, they mutter something like "I had no idea." Right. *I had no idea how crazy you are, James.*

I got infamous writing mysteries, so here's the big mystery plot for this book: How did a shy, introspective kid from a struggling upstate New York river town who didn't have a lot of guidance or role models go on to become, at thirty-eight, CEO of the advertising agency J. Walter Thompson North America? How did this same person become the bestselling writer in the world? That's just not possible.

But it happened. In part because of something else my grandmother preached early and often—*hungry dogs run faster*.

And, boy, was I hungry.

One thing that I've learned and taken to heart about writing books or even delivering a good speech is to tell stories. Story after story after story. That's what got me here, so that's what I'm going to do. Let's see where storytelling takes us. This is just a fleeting thought, but try not to skim too much. If you do, it's the damn writer's fault. But I have a hunch there's something here that's worth a few hours. It has to do with the craft of storytelling.

One other thing. When I write, I pretend there's someone sitting across from me—and I don't want that person to get up until I'm finished with the story.

Right now, that person is you.

let's start with
something crazy

five years at a cuckoo's nest

MY WRITING CAREER unofficially began at McLean Hospital, the psychiatric affiliate of Harvard Medical School in Belmont, Massachusetts. It was the summer of 1965 and I was eighteen. Fresh out of high school. I needed a job, any job, and McLean was hiring. I spent a good part of the next five years at this mental hospital. That's where everything changed about how I saw the world and probably how I saw myself.

I wasn't a patient. I swear. Not that I have anything but the highest regard for mental patients. I just wasn't one of them. Besides, back then I couldn't have afforded a room at McLean, not even space in a double room.

I was a psych aide. I think I was hired because I have empathy for people. You'll be the judge of that. The heart of the job was to talk to patients and, more important, to listen to them. Occasionally, patients tried to hurt themselves. My job was to try and stop that from happening. In addition to my usual daytime shift, I worked two or three overnight shifts a week, from eleven p.m. until seven in the morning. Most nights I just had to watch people sleep. Which isn't that easy.

I had never liked coffee, but I started drinking the awful stuff just to make sure I stayed awake, since there were usually patients on suicide watch at Bowditch or East House in the maximum-security wards where I regularly worked. For hour-long stints I had to sit outside their rooms, watching them flop around in bed, listening to them snore, while I fought off sleep at three or four in the morning.

So I had a lot of free time. I started reading like a man possessed during those long, dark nights of other people's souls.

Two or three times a week, I'd go the three miles or so into Cambridge and make the rounds of the secondhand bookstores. I especially loved tattered, dog-eared books. Books that had been well loved and showed it. The used books cost me a quarter, occasionally a buck, even for thick novels like *The Sot-Weed Factor, The Golden Notebook, The Tin Drum.*

At the time, I wasn't interested in genre fiction, the kind of accessible stuff I write. I had no idea what books were on the *New York Times* bestseller lists. I was a full-blown, know-it-all literary snob—who didn't really know what the hell he was talking about.

My ideas about how the world was supposed to work had been framed growing up in Newburgh, New York, and the somewhat parochial outer reaches of Orange County. As I read novel after novel, play after play, my view of what was possible in life began to change.

That first summer at McLean Hospital, I read a lot of James Joyce and Gabriel García Márquez, plus as much Henry James as I could stomach. I was into playwrights: Samuel Beckett, Harold Pinter, Ionesco, Albee, Israel Horovitz. I read novelists like John Rechy and Jean Genet (*Our Lady of the Flowers* will get you thinking). Also Jerzy Kosinski and Romain Gary. I loved comedic American novelists. Stanley Elkin and Thomas Berger got me laughing out loud. So did Bruce Jay Friedman. John Cheever. Richard Brautigan. Vonnegut.

But the novel that influenced me most was Evan Connell Jr.'s *Mrs. Bridge,* the story of an ordinary middle-class family living in Kansas City. *Mrs. Bridge* is told from the point of view of India Bridge, a wife and mother. A companion novel published ten years later, *Mr. Bridge,* tells the same story from the point of view of Walter, her curmudgeonly lawyer husband. A reviewer in the *New York Times* wrote, "Mr. Connell's novel is written in a series of 117 brief, revealing episodes. The method looks and is rather unusual. . . . It enables any writer who uses it to show, with clarity and compactness, how characters react to representative episodes and circumstances."

Mrs. Bridge and *Mr. Bridge* helped inspire my writing style (don't blame Evan Connell). So did Jerzy Kosinski's novels *Steps* and *The Painted Bird* (don't blame Kosinski). Short chapters. Tight, concise writing (hopefully). Irony and wit (occasionally).

During the time I worked at McLean Hospital, I read everything (except bestsellers, God forbid) I could get my hands on. Then I started scribbling my own short stories, hundreds of them. That was the beginning of the end. I was now officially an addict. I wanted to write the kind of novel that was read and reread so many times the binding broke and the book literally fell apart, pages scattered in the wind.

I'm still working on that one.

cuckoo's nest east

EVERYTHING ABOUT BUSTLING, sometimes over-whelming, Harvard-centric Cambridge, Mass-achusetts, and McLean Hospital, in nearby Belmont, seemed fresh and new, and the experience woke me from what felt like an eighteen-year coma, or at least a very deep sleep.

What made McLean most interesting were the patients.

James Taylor was a patient at McLean. The musician checked himself in for depression as a prep-school senior and stayed for ten months. He wrote "Knocking 'Round the Zoo" about his time at McLean. His breakout hit, "Fire and Rain," was a sad, beautiful tribute to a friend from that time of his life who'd killed herself.

And Taylor definitely was Sweet Baby James.

Long blond hair, stunningly handsome, musician, poet. His sister, Kate, was also a patient at McLean. So was his brother Livingston. Both Kate and Liv also went on to record albums. There was actually a small school on the grounds of McLean and I sometimes escorted Liv or Kate to classes. My only experience with James was hearing him sing several times in the hospital coffee shop. Free admission, good acoustics, great seats ten feet from Sweet Baby James himself.

The poet Robert Lowell checked into McLean twice while I was working there. Lowell would do private readings in his room for an audience of three or four patients and staff.

He would read his poems and occasionally explain what he was trying to accomplish in them or complain about the hospital food or that he wasn't admired enough by some critics and peers he respected.

Lowell was just another crazy guy, but a bright and interesting one. We were friendly, and I found him to be a sweet, generous man. I sat in on as many of his readings as I could.

Hell, I was getting paid to listen to James Taylor and Robert Lowell.

Susanna Kaysen was a patient on South

Belknap, which housed young women who weren't violent. She wrote her memoir *Girl, Interrupted* (which became a hit movie) based on her experiences at McLean. My opinion is that Susanna made up some parts of the story, stretched the truth, anyway, but isn't that what we writers do?

The summer that I worked on the hospital's male maximum-security ward, Bowditch, a Brandeis University premed student named Marty Cohen was a patient. Marty and I became close friends that summer. He was a suicide risk, and it was actually kind of nerve-racking to be his friend.

Late in the summer, several of the patients on Bowditch got to spend a long weekend with the nurses, aides, and a couple of doctors at a camp that had just closed to the public for the season. For some reason that I didn't completely understand at the time, this trip was thought to be therapeutic. It was definitely going to be interesting. One Flew Over the Cuckoo's Nest Goes to Summer Camp.

The camp was on the north shore of a beautiful lake in southern New Hampshire, and late one afternoon I went on a canoe ride with Marty. We stopped paddling and talked pretty much nonstop for an hour or so, like we always did. Only this time, it was out in the middle of a dark blue lake surrounded by birch and balsam firs and rapidly deepening shadows.

There was no breeze. The water was still. The world seemed silent and serene.

Finally, Marty looked at me and quietly asked, "Jim, don't you find it strange that the doctors let a suicide risk like me come out on a lake in a boat like this with you?"

He saw the fear in my eyes and quickly said, "I would *never* do that to you."

I loved Marty for saying that.

A year later, when he was back at Brandeis, Marty killed himself. I still haven't gotten over that. I'm still thinking about Marty—and writing about him.

double specials

ONE AFTERNOON WHEN I arrived for the three-to-eleven shift, I saw that hospital maintenance had put new windows in at the nurses' station on the maximum-security ward. Maria Ruocco was the charge nurse, and a good friend. "What's with the windows?" I asked.

Maria rolled her eyes, but she couldn't hold back a wry smile. "Funny you should ask, James. They're Plexiglas. Hurricane-strength. Won't break. So says the maintenance guy. We'll see."

Case in point—down the hallway was a patient I'll call "Crash." A young guy. Really, really crazy. Crash was on double specials. Regular specials meant that patients were considered a serious risk to themselves or others. These patients needed to have an aide within arm's length at all times. Double specials meant *two* aides within arm's length. That's how dangerous Crash was considered.

As Maria and I stood there at the nurses' station, Crash took off in our direction. Damn the torpedoes, full speed ahead. His two aides followed a half step behind.

"Shit, shit, shit. They're not going to catch him. This is bad! This is bad!"

Maria and I sprinted forward to try and intercept Crash before the inevitable happened. But he got to the new Plexiglas windows first.

Crash crashed headfirst. I'd never heard anything like that sound before. Imagine a melon thrown at full speed against a brick wall. Crash had previously broken three glass windows in the nurses' station. Upon impact with the new Plexiglas window, he dropped to the floor like he'd been shot by a long-distance sniper.

He left us for a moment there, blacked out, maybe gone to heaven for a sneak preview. Then his eyes blinked open. He tried to focus on Maria and I. "Who put those fuckers in? You could hurt somebody."

Just another day at the crazy house, and the three-to-eleven shift was only beginning. I loved my years working at McLean, though. I grew up a lot. Learned to handle responsibility responsibly. Saw rich and poor, business leaders and failing artists, some high-school-age kids completely losing their minds—and, occasionally, finding them again.

I had also started the journey to become a writer. And I thought *they* were the crazy ones.

But hey, I'm getting way, way ahead of myself in this story. Sorry, and I mean it, but I have to go back to the beginning.

Who says you can't go home again?

dirt poor for a while

robert caro or walter isaacson, i'm not

THERE'S SOMETHING I should clarify for you up front. Here's what I'm not going to do in this book. I'm not going to write any more paragraphs like the following one.

My hometown of Newburgh is 4.8 square miles bordered on the east by the Hudson River and on the south by the Hudson Highlands, approximately sixty miles north of Manhattan. Newburgh has its share of significant addresses. From his headquarters on Liberty Street, George Washington, in April 1783, announced the end of the Revolutionary War—and the beginning of America. On Montgomery Street, Thomas Edison built a generating plant that electrified the city in 1884. Off Cochecton Turnpike, the Brook-side Drive-In Theater was a regional destination where seven hundred cars could park in view of a two-thousand-square-foot screen mounted on a seventy-foot tower. I was born in Newburgh and lived on North Plank Road, Gidney Avenue, and North Street before my father changed jobs and our family was uprooted to the Common-wealth of Massachusetts.

That's all factual, yes, but this is a book of true stories the way I remember them. I'm sure I'll get a few things wrong. But I *was* five foot eleven in high school, and I *could* dunk a basketball the summer before my senior year. I *did* take that joy ride I'll tell you about later. And the first girl I ever kissed was named Veronica Tabasco.

I wasn't a big reader in grammar or high school. Sometimes that shows in my prose. My mother and father were readers, though. They set a great example. There were open books everywhere in our house, left spread-eagled in the living room, kitchen, even some bath-rooms. That book-in-every-room approach is supposed to be encouraging but it didn't do anything for me, at home or in Catholic school. I had a goofy-high IQ, but the books, essays, and stories they tried to force-feed us in class were especially boring to me and seemed irrelevant to most of us.

So how did I wind up writing, and reading,

so many books? I'm going to try to tell you how it happened. As I said early on, this is a mystery story.

Actually, come to think of it, quite a few people die.

you're slipping, james

ACCORDING TO PATTERSON family lore, on March 22, 1947, I nearly died at birth at St. Luke's Hospital in Newburgh, New York. I don't remember, but I did live to tell about it.

Let's start with my father. Charles Henry Patterson was a quiet but tough man who came from tough times and from a tough river town.

My dad grew up in the Newburgh poorhouse (think about that for a second or two). It was called the Pogie. His mom was the charwoman there. She cleaned the kitchens and bathrooms, worked, she said, from "seven to seven, seven days a week." For her long, hard work, she and my father got to share a single room on the basement floor. They weren't homeless, but they were damn close. My father never met his father, at least not as far as he could remember.

My mother, Isabelle Ann, attended high school with my dad. After college she became a fourth-grade teacher at St. Patrick's, one of the four Catholic schools in Newburgh. She made next to nothing. Maybe even a little less than that. I'm surprised the parish priests didn't ask her to pay them for the privilege of teaching at their school. Several nights a week, she would be bent over the dining-room table grading papers until nine or ten.

She had a cool mission as a teacher: she wanted to turn mirrors into windows. She pretty much followed the same philosophy at home. Mirrors, physical or symbolic, weren't big in the Patterson house.

My sisters — Mary Ellen, Carole, and Teresa — ruled the roost. In their view of the world, I was hired help. I was muscle. I was their minion. So I handled the garbage detail, the lawn work, the snow removal, and the repair of bicycles, small electrical appliances, deflated balls of all sizes and shapes. We were a very ball-sy family.

I was always a good student, driven to be number one in, well, *everything*, but I'd get a ninety-seven on a test and my mom or dad would say, "How come you didn't get a hundred? You're slipping, James."

The idea I had growing up—and I held on to it into my forties—was that my folks only cared about me as long as I was number one in my class. I don't blame them, because I feel they were doing the best that they could. I think they honestly believed the next Great Depression was just around the corner, and they always clung to *Careful. Careful. Go slow. Look both ways. Then look again. Your best isn't good enough. You're slipping, James.*

my favorite dad story

A FEW WEEKS before my father got shipped out to fight in World War II, he received a long-distance phone call that turned into a famous story in our family. He must have told this one to my sisters and me a couple dozen times.

The man who phoned my father identified himself as George Hazelton from Port Jervis, a town about forty miles from Newburgh. He asked my dad to bear with him for a moment. He needed to set the scene. George told my dad he was about to leave for the Pacific theater with the navy. After dinner the night before, his mother and father had sat him down in the living room. They'd teared up and had trouble speaking.

Finally, his father managed to say, "George, you know we love you very much, and you're about to go off to fight in this horrible war, so we have to tell you something that we've kept from you all these years. We're not your natural parents. We adopted you when you were one year old."

Then George Hazelton told my father—over the phone—*that he was his brother*.

Great punch line, Uncle George. What's that line from the Doobie Brothers song "Takin' It to the Streets"? "You don't know me but I'm your brother."

So Charles Patterson and George Hazelton, two brothers who still hadn't actually met, both went off to fight for their country in World War II.

Miraculously, they both also came home. They became best friends, extremely loyal and loving toward one another. The thing I remember best about the two of them was that when they were together, they would laugh and laugh. And my father didn't laugh all that much.

My father would sometimes tear up when he told the story about how he and his big brother, George, found one another. I think it was the only time I ever saw him cry.

i don't even know
grandpa patterson's first name

A FEW YEARS after the war ended, my uncle George called my father again. This time he started with the punch line: *"I found our father."*

My uncle went on to report that their father was tending bar in Poughkeepsie, New York. He was working in a seedy joint under the Mid-Hudson Bridge. My uncle George said, "C'mon, Pat, let's go to Poughkeepsie. The two of us. I want to meet him."

My father said, "Well, I don't. I'm not interested in meeting the bastard. I'm not going with you, George."

So my uncle went all by himself to this ugly little gin mill sitting under the Poughkeepsie bridge. A couple of rummies were inside, bellied up to the bar. The joint reeked of months-old stale beer and hard liquor that was even older. Just right for a scene in a novel about upstate

New York by William Kennedy or Richard Russo.

My uncle George didn't drink, so he ordered a Coca-Cola. Then he sat there nursing his soda, watching his father, who he'd never met, growing so disgusted by this poor excuse for a human being that he never even introduced himself. After half an hour—an excruciating time, I imagine—Uncle George left the bar and drove back to Port Jervis alone. His father never knew that one of his sons had been there.

And to this day, I don't know my grandpa Patterson's first name.

Small-town bars actually played a big part in my youth. On many a Saturday afternoon, my father would drag me along to a local joint on Broadway in Newburgh. My dad called it "babysitting the boy."

Here was our ritual: The bartender would slap half a mug of beer down in front of me. I was five or six years old. I'd quaff the beer in one big sip. Every Saturday. The guys in the bar would cheer for me, and my dad was clearly proud. Somehow, I didn't become an alcoholic, but encouraging your kid to chug down beers at six was an interesting way of being a dad. I don't recommend it.

the altar-boy story

SOMEHOW I MADE it through those early bar-room days and headed into St. Patrick's grammar school in Newburgh.

I grew up Catholic. Lord, did I grow up Catholic. The Church was all-seeing, all-knowing, omnipresent, and all-powerful. From ages eight through twelve, I was an altar boy. I felt like I had no choice, no free will, and no say in the matter.

This is no exaggeration — I served Mass every day for a year and a half. If there happened to be a funeral, I would serve two Masses that day.

St. Patrick's Catholic Church was about a mile and a half from our house on North Street in Newburgh. Every morning I would ride my bike to church down either Grand or Liberty Street, past beautiful old houses — Federal,

Gothic, Revival, Italianate structures. Or, if I was feeling extra-guilty about something, usually "impure thoughts," I'd walk.

The altar boys at St. Patrick's were mostly good-natured small-town kids. Sometimes, though, we needed to break the rigid rules. *Bless me, Father, for I have sinned. You won't believe this one!*

You really won't. Before and after Mass, we used to snack on *unconsecrated* hosts. (In the Catholic Church, this is almost like eating Jesus.) Those paper-thin communion wafers weren't exactly potato chips but there was a bad-boy thrill to munching them. Of course, no bad deed goes unpunished. The Church was all-seeing, after all.

One morning, I was serving early Mass with a pal named Ray Cosgrove. Halfway through the service, I almost had a kid heart attack.

Communion wafers, at least a dozen of them, were scattered on the floor all around the altar.

God, please have mercy on me!

I immediately figured out what had happened. Ray Cosgrove must've stuffed communion hosts into a pants pocket—with a hole in it. The priest, Father Brennan, who was well over six feet tall and at least two hundred fifty pounds, spotted the hosts and figured he had spilled them. Okay, that gave Ray Cosgrove and I some hope.

He stopped the Mass—which in those days was delivered in Latin.

I was about to have my second kid heart attack of the morning.

This mammoth priest got down on his puffy, arthritic hands and knees. He proceeded to pick up every host, every potential "Body of Christ," then sprinkle holy water all over the floor. This excruciating cleansing ordeal took close to ten minutes.

I held my breath and wondered if *all* the wafers had fallen out of Ray's pocket or if there were more. Would a telltale trail of communion wafers lead right to the guilty ones, Ray Cosgrove and me?

Meanwhile, I was having a more urgent thought: *I will die after this Mass. First, I will be excommunicated by this priest. Then my father will kill me. My mother will help. My sisters will joyfully pitch in—the little witches.*

But Father Brennan never figured things out, and Ray Cosgrove and I sure weren't going to confess our sins to him.

Not to that priest. Not to anyone.

Not until now.

Bless me, reader, I ate the unconsecrated communion hosts.

kissing veronica tabasco

LET'S GET BACK to those "impure thoughts." Or, better yet, some "impure actions."

When I was in sixth grade, I got invited to an elementary-school make-out party. This freaked me out—*the Church was all-seeing, and so were my parents.* But there was no way I was going to say no. Hell, I'd never been kissed by a girl before.

The party of a lifetime was happening after school at the house of one of the girls from my class at St. Patrick's. Her parents both worked. There was no chance they would come home early. We were on our own until three that afternoon. Until three, anything was possible. But what did that even mean, *anything was possible?*

There were six girls and six boys. A lot of staring down at our sneaks or saddle shoes.

Nervous smiles. Giggling. Offers of soda pop. And beer.

We got paired off in no particular order, at least none that I was told about or could figure out.

I slowly walked to a bedroom with a pretty girl named Veronica Tabasco. What a great name for a first-kiss girl, right? Veronica was one of the smart kids in our class. She stuck to her ideas no matter what the nuns said, which I loved about her.

She pulled down the shades in the bedroom. We both laughed. (I think I laughed.) We didn't know what we were doing but our make-out session was kind of sweet. She was a good kisser. She said I was too. I thanked Veronica and she thanked me. What can I say—we were polite St. Patrick's Catholic School students, after all.

The story doesn't end there. Years later, when I was in my early thirties, I went to visit my grandfather's grave at the Calvary Cemetery on the outskirts of Newburgh. (This was my grand-father on my mother's side, "Pop.")

I wasn't that big on visits to cemeteries, and I couldn't remember exactly where the gravesite was, but I finally found it. I stood there, hat in hand, a stiff Hudson River wind chilling me to the bone, and I had a few good memories of Pop. I said a half-remembered prayer or two.

Then I turned back in the direction of my car and—*Jesus*—I read the name on the gravestone right next to my grandfather's.

It was Veronica Tabasco. My first-kiss girl. My sixth-grade crush. According to the stone tablet, Veronica had died in her mid-twenties. I'd had no idea until that moment. It kind of broke my heart.

taking piano lessons
from a nun in a convent

MY INSTINCTS ARE usually pretty good about what I should do—and what I should run away from as fast as possible.

This was true even when I was a kid. I was faced with a dilemma: I was being forced to take piano lessons at Mount St. Mary's Convent with an elderly nun, Sister Catherine Dominica, but even though Sister Catherine Dominica was actually pretty nice (she gave her students, good or bad, gingersnaps after every session), the lessons were truly nasty. The experience rivaled listening to Liberace or watching *The Lawrence Welk Show* on TV. And I knew for sure this was not the road to becoming the next piano-banging Jerry Lee Lewis or Little Richard.

I can still vividly remember the numbing boredom of repeating scales and the tedium of memorizing not one, not two, but three different versions of "Ave Maria." And I actually *liked* "Ave Maria"! All three versions.

I have a decent Irish tenor voice, so I sang a little in the church choir in those days. But I couldn't handle piano lessons at the convent plus endless practice on the *tone-death* spinet in our living room. I finally told my mother I'd had it.

My grandfather leaned into the conversation and said I'd always regret not learning how to play the piano. He was right. Pop was usually right. He also told me to stand up with my back straight or I'd always walk with a slouch.

Today, I walk with a slouch. And I can't play the piano.

Even though I gave up on the piano, I never gave up on music. Back when I was growing up, I was a big Elvis fan. Here's an Elvis story.

We used to have family get-togethers in the summer. My father and his brother, the famous Uncle George, rented a cottage on a small lake and we would all bunk in together for a week or two. I would cajole my cousin Patty, who was two days older than me and a real sweetheart, to walk a mile and a half with me to a lakeside candy store just so I could play Elvis Presley songs on the jukebox. I think I got three plays for a dime. I remember that "Don't Be Cruel" and "Hound Dog" were on the same 45. So were "Teddy Bear" and "Treat Me Nice." And I still believe "Love Me Tender" is a great love song.

Elvis was controversial in those days, especially at our house. The swivel hips, the sensuous lips, the whole sexy-man vibe. If you were a Catholic kid, listening to Elvis was a no-no. Even so, one year I collected Elvis Presley cards. You got a pack of cards and a slab of bubble gum with a mysterious white powder all over it. When my mother found out, she shamed me into throwing my Elvis cards out. She said they were sinful and told me I should confess to a priest about the Elvis trading cards. So I did.

The priest said, "Who doesn't like Elvis Presley?"

My mother.

the moviegoer

MY MOM USED to get rid of me and my sister Mary Ellen by packing us off to the movie theater for Saturday-afternoon double features. To this day, I go to the movies two or three times a week. It's an astonishingly dumb habit. There aren't two or three good movies in a given month. There are usually none. But still I go. Or I did until COVID shut down all the movie theaters.

Back in ancient times, the 1950s, Newburgh had three movie houses—the Ritz, the Academy, and the Broadway—all within a block and a half. Mary Ellen and I were absolutely forbidden to go to the Academy. It was an all-wood structure, and my mother was petrified it would burn down with the two of us trapped inside. In 1956, the Academy actually did burn to the ground. Mary Ellen and I were at the Ritz that day. *Close, you fire gods, but no burned-to-a-crisp Patterson children.*

As a family, the Pattersons would crowd into the old Pontiac and go to the drive-in once or twice a month. The Brookside and Balmville drive-ins had triple features on Friday and Saturday nights. It was two or three bucks *per car,* whether your station wagon had one passenger or ten. The show started at dusk and went until three or four in the morning. The Pattersons would stay for all three movies. If there were a drive-in near where I live now, I'd probably still be game once a month.

My sadness about Hollywood is that most of the films based on my books haven't been very good. Maybe it's the fault of the books. Nah. I believe that *Maximum Ride, The Black Book, The Last Days of John Lennon,* and, especially, *The Noise* would be hugely entertaining films in the right hands. *Middle School: The Worst Years of My Life* was a pretty good family movie. And of course, Morgan Freeman, who played Alex Cross in the movies of *Kiss the Girls* and *Along Came a Spider,* is great in anything. Except maybe *Lucky Number Slevin.*

I've talked to the writer Michael Connelly a few times about how Hollywood has treated his books. He didn't much like *Blood Work,* even though it was directed by Clint Eastwood. On the other hand, the TV series *Bosch* and the movie they made from his novel *The Lincoln Lawyer* turned out really well. So I'm jealous of Michael. Hell, I love movies a lot more than he does!

Just once—*once*—I'd like to stand up and cheer for one of my books up on the silver screen.

I had a good talk with the excellent screenwriter Eric Roth recently. Roth wrote *Forrest Gump, Munich,* and *A Star Is Born,* and he was interested in my book *The Last Days of John Lennon.* Eric asked me what I wanted out of the movie. I told him, "I love movies. I just want to be proud of one film with my name on it somewhere. Below yours, of course, Eric."

the first color tv

SINCE THE CORONAVIRUS outbreak, we've heard a lot of praise for workers as heroes, which I think is a good thing. It's why I decided to write the nonfiction bestseller *ER Nurses.* Our nurses definitely are mega-heroes, real-life ones.

When I was growing up, blue-collar workers weren't necessarily seen as heroes but there was more respect for them, more respect for the work itself. A lot of people felt lucky just to have a job. Feeding your family was considered noble. It was in our house, anyway.

My grandparents Nan and Pop—my mother's parents—didn't have much money, but they somehow managed to buy one of the first color TVs in our part of Newburgh. Color TV turned out to be both a small miracle and a mess.

On Sundays, a dozen or so friends and neighbors would come over and join our family to watch color TV pretty much ruin one of our favorite shows, *Bonanza*. Suddenly the Cartwright family's faces were all the same shade of scarlet red; landscapes were streaked lime green and blue. But everybody who was crowded into the living room cheered at the beginning and end of every show. My sisters were all in love with the curly-haired actor Michael Landon, who played "Little Joe" Cartwright. So was my grandmother.

Nan was also a die-hard fan of wrestling and roller derby. She made me and my sister Mary Ellen watch roller derby every Saturday morning. We didn't much like the derby, but we loved being with Nan.

Nan had a commonsense solution for just about any problem. When my sister Mary Ellen and I worried ourselves sick because our cat got stuck up in a tree, Nan told us, "No need to call the fire department. You ever see a cat skeleton up in a tree?" That was Nan.

Nan's parents—my *great*-grandparents the Zelvises—were addicted to TV soap operas. Not long after they got their first TV, we went to visit them at their home on lovely tree-lined Benkard Avenue, which nowadays is the scene of gang wars.

When Great-Grandma Zelvis opened the front door, she was weeping. Inside the house, my great-grandfather Walter Zelvis, who had escaped from Russia to avoid the military draft, was also crying. Suddenly, everybody was hugging everybody else, though my sisters and I had no idea why.

Eventually, Great-Grandma Zelvis was able to regain some of her composure. A tough Lithuanian lady, she told us what had brought on the tears. "Johnny Monte died. Ohhh, ohhh, Johnny Monte is dead. Ohhh, poor Johnny Monte. Poor Johnny!"

We were all still baffled. Who the heck was Johnny Monte? Must be somebody we didn't know in the building. Oh, well, too bad about poor Johnny Monte. We should say a prayer, light a candle; maybe I'd toast Johnny Monte with a stolen communion wafer.

Turns out, there was no Johnny Monte living on Benkard Avenue or anywhere in Newburgh. Johnny Monte was a character on one of their TV soap operas. My great-grandparents saw him die on TV and didn't understand that he wasn't actually dead. So they mourned his loss. They believed everything they heard or saw on TV. Amazingly, that kind of thing is still going on today—and sometimes it still makes you want to cry.

let's play some ball

IN MY "YEAR of growing dangerously"—I think I was twelve—I sprouted six inches so quickly, I had to stay in bed for over a week to recover. Suddenly, I was five foot eleven and going on six feet in a hurry. I became a scary Little League pitcher, a center on the CYO basketball team, the tallest kid in my class.

I bet my father a dollar that I would be six feet by year's end. I *never* got to six feet. And I reneged on the bet.

Playing sports got me through the Newburgh years. Later in life, I took up the diabolical game of golf. I now have nine holes in one. The ninth came this year—*on my birthday*. A good friend told me that should be the opening line of this book. Obviously, I didn't agree. But I was definitely tempted.

As a kid, I played stickball, baseball, basketball, flag football. I was pretty good—of course, most guys say that, so, fine, let's go to the highlight reel.

The summer between my junior and senior years in high school, I dunked a basketball a dozen times. Honest. I don't care what my asshole friends say. In baseball, I had a good fastball and a slider.

When I was ten, I didn't get picked for any Little League team and I was crushed. Absolutely heartbroken. I'm not kidding. I cried walking off the field that day. The next year, at eleven, I'd become a good hitter and pitcher and wound up as Little League home-run champ two years in a row.

At twelve, I was really big for a Little League pitcher. I was also scary-fast—and scary-wild. I even had a little peach fuzz on my chin.

Speaking of peach fuzz, there was a variety store near our school—Jockey Joe's—that sold beer to underage kids. Since I had the chin fuzz, I was the one who got to buy the beer.

Jockey Joe was this mean little bugger who reportedly had a gun and definitely kept a baseball bat behind the counter at his corner store. He was also a small-time, small-town bookie.

But he sold us beer. No problem with it. The only ID "proof" we needed was a dollar bill. Four quarters would do fine.

Sometimes I'd mumble, "It's for my dad." Jockey Joe wouldn't have cared if the beer was for my baby sister.

After I made the buy, my pals and I—I'm not going to rat them out here—would head up to Downing Park and down the beers, two to a man.

Back to sports. My friend Mickey Fescoe was a very good high-school athlete. He finally admitted, at age seventy, that back in the day, he'd been scared to hit against me because I was so big and fast and as wild as the old Yankees reliever Ryne Duren, who was the model for Charlie Sheen's character in *Major League*.

When I was fourteen, we had a strong Pony League team, the Orioles. I was a pitcher, and the catcher was a kid named Pudge. He and his brother, who was two years older, came from Wallkill, a nearby farm town. Pudge was a good catcher who was crazy-competitive and a major ball-breaker. We were fourteen years old and he was already chewing tobacco. He'd be behind home plate, chewing his tobacco wad, spitting the brown goop into the dirt between pitches.

The first time Pudge and I met, Pudge talked at me between tobacco chews. "I'll catch you bare-handed, Jim Patterson. Don't even need a glove. My brother throws harder than you with his left hand—and he's right-handed." Pudge and I went on to become friendly—not friends, but we tolerated one another and we won a lot of baseball games.

I was one of the better pitchers in the league and Mickey Fescoe was definitely the best hitter. But neither of us got picked for the all-star team—which pissed the hell out of Mickey. Yeah, and me too.

Pretty dejected, the two of us were sitting in the stands, squinty-eyed, watching an in-field drill before our all-star team played a team from another county. The kid pitching for us, Mickey Scott, was a year younger than Fescoe and I. He wasn't that great in Pony League—but Mickey Scott wound up playing for the Yankees. So I guess Bo Gill, who ran the league and was also the sportswriter for the *Newburgh News,* could spot talent better than we could.

Bo Gill was bald as a cue ball and kind of a dumpy, funny-looking guy. The day of the all-star game, he wanted everything to look picture-perfect. As he was bent over, dusting off home plate, an infielder threw a ball and it hit Bo on the crown of his head. Knocked him right on his butt.

Fescoe and I couldn't stop laughing. It was a Keystone Cops physical-comedy scene—very funny. Until we spotted Bo Gill's wife. Mrs. Gill was sitting directly behind us, watching us laugh as her husband went tumbling onto his rear.

The very cool thing was, she started laughing too.

Bo, if you're reading this in "the good place," here's to you—but this is definitely sweet revenge for keeping me and Fescoe off your all-star team. You know the saying: *Revenge is a dish best served cold.* I have to admit, it is a tasty dish.

play hard or go home

GROWING UP, I had zero interest in being a writer. Almost all the books I was forced to read in school completely turned me off. The only novelist I knew with a connection to my hometown was the crime writer Mickey Spillane. Spillane had a big house on nearby Orange Lake and I'd seen him a couple of times in Lentini's restaurant. My father was a fan and got Mickey Spillane's autograph at the bar there. Not me. I had no interest in mystery novels.

My high-school friends figured I'd become a big-deal doctor or lawyer, which was about as good as it got in Newburgh. Not so bad, really. None of them imagined I'd become a writer. Honestly, I thought I'd probably be a doctor or lawyer myself. Probably a lawyer, since I don't like the sight of blood. And yeah, I see the irony in that.

But my passion in those days was basketball. I played pretty much winter, spring, and summer. Didn't matter if there was a blizzard or if the temperature was close to 100. As Skee-Lo would later sing in "I Wish": "I was a little bit taller—I wish I was a baller."

One of my favorite life lessons took place on a Newburgh playground's basketball court when I was in eighth grade. Actually, I think I'd just finished eighth grade. I was playing in a pickup game against a team that included the star guard for the Newburgh high-school team, the county champs.

I was in grade school but good enough to play on the same court with the seventeen- and eighteen-year-olds. But that afternoon the star high-school kid crushed me. He blocked my shots, drove right through me, didn't take it easy on me just because I was fourteen.

After the game, he bought me a soda and sat down next to me. He said something I'll never forget. "Look, when we're out there on the court, I'm going to beat the living shit out of you. Which is what I just did, right? But when the game's over, we go and have a soda."

I've always thought that was a great lesson about sports and a whole lot of other things in life. You play hard, you do your best, but in the end, have enough perspective to know it's a game. If you're a Yankees fan, you don't actually hate Red Sox fans.

Well, maybe it's okay to hate the Red Sox. Or the Yankees. Or Tom Brady. Nah. You can't hate the GOAT. That's "Greatest of All Time" for all of you non–ESPN fans.

"i know you better than you know yourself"

BROTHER LEONARD, THE Christian Brothers principal at St. Patrick's High School, had a divine plan for me. "I know you better than you know yourself," he liked to say. Not that the saying made a lot of sense to any of us. Then again, Brother Leonard was fond of declaring, in complete seriousness, things like "Hey, I misunderstood me."

Some of you will find this next part hard to believe—but it happened.

In my senior year I applied to Harvard, Yale, Colby, and Bates. As of February, I hadn't heard back from any of the schools. As background, you need to understand that my family didn't know much or think much about college. But my mother finally set up an appointment for us to talk to Brother Leonard about the admissions situation.

I already had a theory about what was about to go down.

The good brother kept my mother and me waiting in the school cafeteria (which offered a daily choice of hot dogs or hamburgers for our school lunches. That was it: hamburger or hot dog, every day). Finally, he called us to his office. He listened as my mom and I told him our concerns. Then he told us the deal he'd made on our behalf.

"Oh, I never sent your transcript to any of those schools. I only sent it to Manhattan College." Manhattan College was run by the same group of Christian Brothers who taught at St. Patrick's. So, of course, Manhattan was a Catholic school. "Here's the good news, Mrs. Patterson. James has been accepted at Manhattan with a full scholarship. You'll never have to pay a cent. Congratulations."

Then the principal shook hands with both of us. That sanctimonious son of a bitch. I wanted to smack him. I wanted to scream in his face.

But that was that. As always, I had the sense that Brother Leonard felt God was sitting on his shoulder doing the actual decision-making. To this day, I have a problem with authority figures. Brother Leonard is the reason why.

I immediately applied to Hamilton College and was accepted—but with no financial aid. My father told me I could head on down to the bank and take out a big personal loan for college. He had no problem if that was my decision, but it meant going down to the bank *by myself*.

So off I went to Manhattan College, which, by the way, happens to be in the Bronx.

Before I take leave of my hometown, I have to say that, to this day, I look at the world through the lens of a blue-collar kid who grew up in Newburgh. It's a blessing. I think it's why I've never been too full of myself, too impressed with bestseller lists. It's probably why I'm kind of a working-class storyteller. I just keep chopping wood.

unpublished

living in the big city

IN THE FALL I arrived at Manhattan College. It turned out to be a terrific experience that helped mold and shape me into whatever the hell I am today.

Manhattan's liberal arts curriculum was disciplined and also demanding. In my class there were two of the top kids from Regis High School in New York City. At that time, Regis was one of the most prestigious Catholic high schools in the country. During my freshman year, I found out that those Regis kids had wound up at Manhattan College pretty much the same way I had. Their parents wanted them at a Catholic college. We all got hijacked. End of discussion—if there had ever even been a discussion.

Years later, when I was working in advertising, I'd sometimes get asked how I survived in such a tough, competitive business. I'd usually shrug and say the ad world was nothing compared to high school and college under the Christian Brothers.

Before I get off the subject of the Christian Brothers, here's one more story about Catholic-school education that folks today—especially kids—might find impossible to believe. But it happened.

At St. Patrick's High School, we had the same Christian Brother for math and science my junior and senior years. Class always started the same way. Brother Henry—Hank—a big Polish guy with a full head of wavy blond hair and an unnerving smirk, would saunter into class and give the same opening line every day.

"Gentlemen—and I use the term loosely—anyone who doesn't have their homework, please stand."

Now, on most days, I had my homework. I wasn't stupid and I wasn't a masochist. But let's say I didn't have my work one day. Up would come Brother Henry and he would stand directly in front of me. He was six foot three if he was an inch.

Then he would say, "Mr. Patterson, do you know what's going to happen to you now?"

"Yes, Brother." *Hank. You bastard.*

"Do you know why it's going to happen, Mr. Patterson?"

"Yes, Brother." *You sadist.*

Then Hank would swing his huge right hand up from below his waist, fast and hard, and smack me a good one across the face.

Then on to his next victim. "Mr. Hatfield—"

"Yes, Brother. You can skip the preliminaries. Just hit me."

Every single day before math and science class started at St. Patrick's High School.

So, yeah, by comparison, advertising was pretty much a walk in the park on a blue-skied sunny day.

the fightin' irish

IT SHOULD BE clear by now that I'm not telling my story in precise chronological order, so let me jump ahead a bit. Just for a minute or so. After Manhattan College, I got a full-ride PhD fellowship to study English at Vanderbilt. Vanderbilt was terrific—*is* terrific—but honestly, Manhattan College was more competitive and a whole lot tougher. Former New York City mayor Rudy Giuliani went to Manhattan. So did two Southern District of New York DAs, Ronald Ellis and John Keenan. Former New York City police commissioner Ray Kelly is a Manhattan grad. But so is Thomas Gambino, *caporegime* of the Gambino crime family. Hey, it takes all kinds to play cops and robbers.

I will say this: there were a lot of tough kids at Manhattan College. That school definitely got you ready for the real world.

During my first semester at Manhattan, the dean of Arts and Sciences approached me. "Look, James, I know Brother Leonard at St. Patrick's, and I know what happened to you. It shouldn't have happened." The dean offered to make things right. "If you do very well here in your first year, I'll get you into Harvard. That's a promise."

I did very well, but I also made a lot of good friends, and at the end of the first year, I decided to stay at Manhattan.

Years later, I became friends with Frank McLaughlin, who had been an All-American basketball player at another Catholic school, Fordham Prep, and then wound up going to Fordham University. *What a surprise.* He became an assistant basketball coach at Fordham under Digger Phelps, and when Phelps got hired at Notre Dame, Frank traveled to South Bend with him. He eventually left Notre Dame and became the head coach at Harvard.

While Frank was at Harvard, he met legendary North Carolina basketball coach Dean Smith. Smith blew Frank's mind by telling him that when he was at Fordham Prep, Smith had gone there personally to recruit him. Dean Smith wanted him at North Carolina, which had one of the best basketball programs in the country. You know, the school where Michael Jordan played. "But the Jesuits wouldn't let me get anywhere near you. They made sure you were going to Fordham."

Of course they did, Frank. They knew you would lose your immortal soul at the University of North Carolina.

One footnote to the Frank McLaughlin story. When I was a freshman in high school, my family moved across the Hudson from Newburgh to Beacon, New York. Our house was next door to Phelps's Funeral Home, which was owned by Digger Phelps's father. The funeral home was how Coach Phelps got the nickname "Digger."

I met Dick Phelps years later and he said he liked the Alex Cross novels. I told him I always rooted for Notre Dame and that I'd once had a crush on his sister. Digger said, "You stay away from my sister."

"Digger, she's like fifty now."

"Yeah, so what? Stay away from my sister."

sucker-punched

MY SOPHOMORE YEAR at Manhattan, I played in a very competitive men's basketball league in the Bronx. Our team was made up of Manhattan students who had played high-school or some college ball and we were undefeated. Exams being what they were, only five of us made it to one of the playoff games.

A wiseass on the other team figured that if he took one of us out, we'd have to forfeit the game and would get knocked out of the play-offs. So he sucker-punched me, knocking out two of my front teeth and breaking my nose. I have to admit, it was a hell of a punch.

I arrived at Misericordia Hospital around ten that night. The room I shared looked out on a local cemetery. Nice view. Cheery.

I couldn't breathe through my broken nose, and when I tried to breathe through my mouth, the pain put me over the moon. A nerve in the stump of one of my broken teeth was exposed. That made for a very bad night for me somewhere in the Bronx.

The next morning, a doctor who looked to be in his mid-seventies but was still gigantic stopped by. I told him, "I'm having a little bit of a tough time here. My nose is stopped up. When I breathe through my mouth it *hurts*."

"So don't breathe," the doctor joked. Not that funny to me, but he thought he was the next George Carlin.

But then he hustled me down into the bowels of Misericordia Hospital. He led me into a dusty stockroom crammed with boxes of hospital supplies. Then, I swear to God, he grabbed a pair of pliers.

"I'm going to yank out that loose piece of your tooth," he announced.

I was thinking, *This sounds like a really bad idea*. But I let him try plan A because he was a doctor. My problem with authority figures had never extended to doctors. To this day, it doesn't. (Whatever my good friend Dr. Bruce Moskowitz tells me to do, *I do*.)

So anyway, my "Doctor in the Bronx" used his pliers to grab hold of the remaining fragment of my tooth. He yanked really hard. I heard this stomach-turning crunching noise and then this huge doctor goes spinning across the stockroom. He looked down at his pliers and gave me the news: "Didn't get it."

He headed back toward me with his trusty pliers. Maybe that's where I came up with one of the bad guys in *Kiss the Girls*. But, hey, the doctor got the tooth—on the third try. Then he told me, "James, put it under your pillow for the Tooth Fairy."

writing 101

I REMEMBER THIS as if it happened just the other day. It was 1968, a brutal, heartbreaking, soul-searching year. Martin Luther King Jr. and Robert Kennedy were murdered. Richard Nixon defeated Hubert Humphrey. Vietnam was on fire. I think it was something about that confusing, terrifying time that got me thinking seriously about trying to be a writer, trying to get some truth out of my head and down on paper.

I had begun scribbling short stories while I was working summers at McLean Hospital. In college, I wrote fiction every single day. Mostly short stories but a couple of plays. I was hooked. I was an unrepentant junkie. I couldn't stop writing if I wanted to.

Nowadays, people ask me what they should do to become a writer. I usually tell them that if it's meant to be, they won't really have a choice. The writing just takes over everything. You think about writing all day, every day. And most important—you actually write.

I had to sit through the dreaded required writing course at Manhattan. It was for two credits. A breather. Everybody who showed up got an A or a B. The professor who taught it was a well-intentioned layman who was the Catholic poet laureate, whatever the hell that was. I had written a couple of stories for the college literary magazine. This professor felt compelled to tell me, "You write well enough, *but stay away from fiction.*"

Probably good advice.

But to be honest, my problem with authority figures continued, so screw him. I started writing two, sometimes three, short stories a week.

Something about that early self-training seemed to work out. I think it's still operating okay. Hey, if I can make *my* life story interesting, I can make just about any story line work.

the fillmore east story

A **FRIEND OF** mine at Manhattan got a hundred concert tickets in the mail from the new music venue Fillmore East. *New* as in the place had only been open for a couple of weeks. Problem was, the tickets were for the *previous* weekend's show. Somebody had obviously messed up.

A crafty city kid, he took the tickets down to the Fillmore, on Second Avenue near East Sixth. He made a fuss. "You sent me these goddamn tickets for *last* Saturday and they came on *this* Tuesday. What am I supposed to do with them now?"

The Fillmore honcho he talked to didn't exactly buy the story, but he liked something about my friend, who was a likable enough guy. As they continued to talk, the Fillmore dude offered up a compromise. "If you can deliver eight to ten reliable college kids every week, we'll pay them twelve dollars for the night. They'll work as ushers. Obviously, the ushers get to listen to the music free."

When my friend got back to campus, he gathered up a few students he thought were reliable. I was one of them. For the rest of that year, I ushered at every concert I possibly could.

The work was easy. All I had to do was stumble around in the dark with a flashlight and help stoned hippies find their seats. If somebody was tripping, I'd help out too. I was pretty much an expert at that. Hell, my summer job was working at a mental hospital.

I looked forward all week to going down to the East Village and actually getting paid to hear some of the best rock music in the world.

It got so eardrum-bursting loud some nights I thought I would lose my mind and definitely my hearing, but I loved every minute of it. I don't know if I can explain it but I mentally tried to force my brain up into the back of my head as a protective measure. I was seriously afraid I could go deaf.

One of the acts I saw was Jimi Hendrix. Hendrix was a little out of it—or a little too into it—but definitely not at his best. Still, it was Jimi Hendrix.

Even so, Hendrix wasn't the best thing that happened that night. At the time, nobody had heard of his warm-up act. Nobody knew their songs. The group was Sly and the Family Stone, and that night, they blew Jimi Hendrix away.

I saw the Doors play two shows a night, two nights in a row at the Fillmore. The first night, March 22, was my birthday, one I never forgot. As advertised, Jim Morrison was a genuine madman, but he was incredibly charismatic onstage. It was impossible to take your eyes off him, the way he caressed the mic stand like a lover.

After the Doors' second show on the twenty-third, we twelve-dollar-a-night ushers hung around. I didn't know it at the time, but one of my fellow ushers was the photographer Robert Mapplethorpe, and he'd brought his then girl-friend, singer and poet Patti Smith.

It was after three in the morning, but Morrison and some of the other members of the band stayed to talk with Bill Graham, the music promoter who ran the Fillmore East and Fillmore West.

Graham and the Doors took seats in the

second or third row. Ushers were smoking and tripping a couple of rows behind them.

I believe the Fillmore was once an old vaudeville theater with three or four balconies. Heavy stage lights hung down from the ceiling. I noticed that Morrison was staring up at the ceiling. He stared for a long time.

Then Morrison started getting upset, raising his voice. Suddenly he was yelling at Bill Graham. "That's dangerous, man. Those lights could come crashing down, man! I know they could! Kill everybody in these front rows!"

Bill Graham said, "You're crazy, Jim. Those lights won't come down in a million years."

Morrison got up and wandered off, still yelling at Graham and even at the ushers—which we loved! We were honored that Jim Morrison actually talked to us, even if he was yelling—then, maybe ten minutes later, we all heard screaming coming from somewhere above us.

I looked up and couldn't believe what I was seeing. Morrison was dangling from the fricking stage lights attached to the ceiling. He was swinging from the lights, kicking his long legs, and screaming down at Graham, "You were right, Bill! You were right, man!" I was thinking to myself, *This is going to be the death of Jim Morrison and I'm going to watch him die.*

He didn't, though. Not that night at the Fillmore, anyway. He was saving his swan song for Paris and a pathetic grave at Père Lachaise.

I'm really glad I didn't see Jim Morrison die.

the end of art as i knew it

APPARENTLY, SOMEBODY CHISELED it in stone somewhere that you have to suffer for your art. Especially if your art isn't quite art yet.

But art isn't all suffering.

Junior year at Manhattan, I didn't have classes on Wednesday afternoons.

So I'd ride the subway for forty-five minutes from 242nd Street to the theater district, where half-price tickets—sometimes less than half price—were available for some Broadway matinees (which typically cost $7.50). Other than the monotonous subway trip, I was in heaven, fantasizing that one day—sooner rather than later—I'd write a Broadway play myself. Maybe I'd be the next Sam Shepard or Leonard Melfi.

One snowy winter Wednesday, I went to see

Rosencrantz and Guildenstern Are Dead at the Alvin Theatre on West Fifty-Second Street.

I was totally pumped up to see the play. *Let it snow, let it snow.* The tragicomedy that playwright Tom Stoppard had adapted from *Hamlet* (the title characters in Stoppard's play have minor roles in Shakespeare's) was already famous from its run at London's National Theatre. The reviews were brilliant, and I shook snow out of my hair and entered the theater, thinking, *I'm a young artist. I'm going to be a writer. I can do this.*

I loved the first act. And the second. I was lost in Stoppard's words and the crazy plot to kill Hamlet so that Rosencrantz could marry Ophelia. Meanwhile, seated next to me were two women around my age who I didn't know from Rosencrantz or Guildenstern.

At the start of the third act, one of them reached over and started rubbing my leg.

From the instant of that first gentle rub, I lost all interest in seeing where Stoppard's play went, how it got there, how it ended. All there was were these two women sitting very close to me, one of them stroking my leg. I couldn't have cared less about *Rosencrantz and Guildenstern*—even if it did go on to win eight Tonys.

So much for theater; so much for art. Real life wins every time. Hormones win. To this day, I don't know exactly what happened at the end of *Rosencrantz and Guildenstern Are Dead.* And I don't particularly care.

three days of peace & love & loud music & rain

EVERYBODY MY AGE says they went to Woodstock, but I actually did go.

Working at the Fillmore East had been a real trip, going half deaf listening to Jimi Hendrix, Jefferson Airplane, the Doors, the Dead. But Woodstock was a whole different kind of loud music and freewheeling lifestyle experience. We were going to change the world. Change it for three days that summer, anyway.

Two college friends, Deli Bob Shaw and B. J. Stringer, joined me and about half a million other fools driving or hitchhiking to somebody's farm somewhere in upstate New York's dairy land. City record stores were charging eighteen dollars for advance three-day tickets, but God only knew what the hell "Woodstock" was and what was going to happen in the unlikely event that we actually got there.

We exited the New York State Thruway and got on a skinny dirt road winding slowly to nowhere. Word had spread about Arlo Guthrie's announcement to the gathering crowds: "The New York State Thruway is closed, man."

Meanwhile, traffic on the dirt road had virtually stopped. Then it *did* stop.

So we parked. Just left the old VW there and joined the amped-up crowd, which we hoped was walking in the general direction of Yasgur's Farm in Bethel, New York.

Then, there it was—nirvana. Except that once we actually got to the Woodstock festival, I don't think we were ever closer to the stage than a quarter mile.

There were loudspeakers everywhere and the sound was decent (I think). But we were sure a long, long way from the live acts.

Still, we were there—smack in the middle of all that peace and love.

We listened to gravelly voiced Richie Havens, the great lung-busting Janis Joplin, and crazy-ass Country Joe and the Fish. The only thing missing, my only disappointment, was that John Lennon decided not to appear at Woodstock.

In the late afternoon, it started to rain—and

it rained, and it rained, and it rained some more. And then I think it must've started to rain mud.

Late that first night, I fell asleep on the side of a hill. I woke up because I was sliding down the hill in a river of mud. I was soaked to the skin, probably a little stoned, and I was laughing like a wind-up idiot. That was Woodstock.

We stayed for about a day and a half as it continued to rain. The mud got feet, not inches, deep. My friends and I finally made a group decision: "Okay, well, we did this thing. We were at Woodstock. We made history. It'll be a story someday."

hippie writer in the deep south

HOPING TO SOMEDAY write the Pretty Good American Novel, I applied to graduate English programs and got accepted at Virginia, Vanderbilt, and Indiana.

Indiana had a well-respected English department and a great basketball team under Bobby Knight. Virginia was top-notch on the academic side. But it was a surprise when Vanderbilt offered me a full-ride PhD fellowship. The entire three years was free, plus I'd get a two-hundred-dollar monthly stipend. Back in 1970, two hundred bucks a month went a long way, especially for somebody with beans-and-hot-dog tastes like me.

My Woodstock buddy B. J. Stringer and I decided to tour the South and check out Vanderbilt in Nashville, Tennessee, that summer of '70. I had never even seen the university. No tour, no interview, no nothing.

The two of us had no money either. At least we had a game plan. We were bumming around in this old jalopy, and every third or fourth day, we'd stay in a seedy motel, something that was dirt cheap but didn't bring to mind the shower scene in *Psycho*. The other days, we'd sleep outside because it was too hot to sleep in the car.

Summers in the South, man. Super-muggy and mosquito-y, and sleeping outside sucked. This was also the summer of the movie *Easy Rider*. Remember that one? A couple of dope-smoking, Harley-riding hippies played by Peter Fonda and Dennis Hopper. Spoiler alert: they get beat up with baseball bats.

As two long-haired hippies ourselves, whenever BJ and I slept outdoors that summer, we had continuing nightmares about getting brained by ball bats.

Sometimes sleeping inside was just as spooky. When we finally got to Nashville, we pulled up in front of a homey-looking bed-and-breakfast. When we entered the foyer, we were greeted by a hundred or so of the creepiest mama and baby dolls you'd ever see. But the price was right.

So we double-locked the door in our room. And that night, we traded nightmares featuring fungo bats crushing our skulls for much scarier ones filled with creepy polyvinyl dolls with beady eyes and frozen expressions.

The next day, we toured Vanderbilt and I remember thinking, *Do I really want to go to grad school? How will my long hair go over in Tennessee? Why does everyone I pass on this campus smile and say hello? That's not how we do it in New York.*

But I decided I *did* want to go to grad school, and being a grad student at Vanderbilt wound up being a life-changing event. Vanderbilt was the first place where I enjoyed school. I was reading books and plays that interested me. I had a class in creative writing that was actually creative. *What a concept.* And I made great new Southern friends, like Lynda Cole from Kentucky and Lewis Lavine from Florida.

Unfortunately, it was a long drive from Vanderbilt to my family's new home in Lexington, Massachusetts. I would make the trip without stopping to sleep—twenty-four, twenty-five hours on the road. Which was crazy.

What was even crazier: while I drove, I'd write Broadway musicals in my head.

I would literally make up the musicals. Concept, original songs, lyrics, story line. It was nuts, but at least it kept me awake while I drove. Later, I wished I'd thought about writing the songs down, but at the time I figured, *Nah. I'm not a musician. I'm not a lyricist. I don't play any instruments.* So it didn't seem like fertile ground. And at that point, being totally honest with myself, I didn't believe I could be any kind of writer.

the mystery thickens

GRADUATE SCHOOL AT Vanderbilt was all
English classes, all stories, all novels, all the
time. It was paradise for any reader and even
better for a writer wannabe like me who liked
to spend most of the day making up stories in
his head.

The best course I took at Vandy happened
because I brazenly approached a professor I
liked and admired, gave him a list of thirty
novels I hadn't read yet but was dying to try,
and said, "Let's read some cool books and talk
about them." He bought the idea.

So we picked fifteen novels, and that was the
course. Imagine that. You read books that you
really, really want to read, then you talk about
them with another book lover.

I would read a novel or two a week and then
we'd talk for an hour or more over Dixie beers

in a nearby country-music gin mill. It was great, probably the best experience I ever had in school. In fact, it might be a model for a college English course just about every student would love. It could just as easily work for a class of two hundred and one professor. The students read books they're *aching* to read; the professor talks about big-picture stuff.

The creative-writing course I took with Vanderbilt professor Walter Sullivan was the other highlight for me. Sullivan was a *very* conservative Southern gentleman. He could've had his own show on Fox News these days. I looked like a little hippie, because I *was* a little hippie. I had long hair, a beard, wore bell-bottoms and flip-flops.

But Walter Sullivan loved me—at least, he loved my short stories. He'd read one aloud every other class. The other students probably wanted to kill me, and I couldn't blame them, but I was starting to gain some confidence in my writing for the first time. Sullivan said, "You have the gift. Don't waste it."

I probably did. *Sorry, Walter Sullivan.* You set me on a righteous road, I just didn't take it where you wanted me to go. *I sold out and wrote a bunch of thrillers.*

my time as a trappist monk

VANDERBILT GRAD STUDENTS were given their own carrels hidden deep in the darkened library stacks of Kirkland Hall. Each carrel consisted of a small desk, a gooseneck lamp, and whatever books you were currently reading or just wanted to leave out on your desk to show how smart you were.

On my desk I kept *The Journals of Thomas Merton*. Every time I went to the carrel, I read some Merton. He'd been a student at Columbia when he converted to Catholicism. Maybe *converted* isn't a strong enough word. After Merton left Columbia, he eventually wound up at the Abbey of Our Lady of Gethsemani in Kentucky. Three years later, he took vows to become a Trappist monk. If you're not familiar with the Trappists, basically, they don't talk.

Thomas Merton stayed at the abbey for

twenty-seven years. His autobiography *The Seven Storey Mountain* sold a couple of million copies—a hugely unlikely bestseller about a student who becomes a monk.

During my second semester at Vanderbilt, I was smoking a little too much weed. I finally said to myself, "If you're going to be a writer, you need to get control of your life. Do it. Now. Like, *tomorrow*."

So that weekend, I drove to the Trappist monastery at Gethsemani. I just showed up at the front gates. A couple of the monks would meet deliveries or visitors, and they were allowed to talk to anyone who came to the door.

A very nice, very polite monk spoke to me. He said, "Tell me why you're here, James."

I answered as honestly as I could. "I'm just sort of wandering in space and time. *Lost* might be the right word. I'm not loving the life I'm leading. I think I want to be a writer. I also think that might be an absurd idea. Not sure. I need to think things through. Maybe I need to pray. I read a lot of Thomas Merton. Oh, and I smoke too much pot."

The nice monk gave me a mini-lecture. He said, "Life is like a football game, James. If you run really fast but you step out-of-bounds, well, the touchdown doesn't count."

I couldn't help thinking, *Boy, I wish this nice guy wasn't talking. Where's the vow of silence when you need it?*

Anyway, I got to stay at Gethsemani for eleven days. And, boy, did it straighten my ass out. I committed to trying to become a writer, committed to whatever it would take to make that happen. I basically stopped smoking weed. I think from the time of that self-imposed retreat until now, I've smoked it only two or three times. I'm not judging all the pot smokers out there, even where it's still illegal. I'm just doing what's right for me.

I deflect a lot with humor but I have a very serious side. During my teenage years in Newburgh, I thought a lot about becoming a priest. At Gethsemani I thought about it again. There was a simplicity to life there that was appealing. I wanted to write but I wasn't sure that I could make it. I also wondered whether I was cut out for marriage. My parents fought constantly, so much so that my sisters and I called them "the Bickersons." Would I end up becoming that kind of father and husband? I just didn't know. So I stayed at the monastery longer than I'd planned. And I prayed.

If you stay as a guest at Gethsemani, you don't have to follow any of the rituals, but you can. That's what I did. *Brother James.*

The Trappists go to bed every night around seven thirty. They get up at three thirty in the morning. They go to chapel, pray, then go out to the surrounding fields and do nasty manual labor. They go back to chapel for Mass. They sing a lot of hymns, and, boy, can they sing. The monks all looked like they were in terrific shape, by the way. They eat smart—rice and bread, fresh veggies, a couple of giblets of meat. After breakfast, they go out and work in the fields again.

They pray, they work, they pray again, they sleep. They do this every day, seven days a week. Kind of like the coronavirus shelter-in-place routine. Only worse. But the monks seemed to love it. I rarely saw a long face.

One of the Trappists apparently explained my situation to a priest who was visiting there, a young guy who was questioning whether he wanted to continue to be a priest.

One afternoon, the young priest and I took a walk in the woods. We had a fine talk. I enjoyed his company. He openly talked about the troubles he was having in his parish, which were sexual in nature. I talked about starting a different kind of life for myself. At a certain point, deep in the woods, the priest said, "Can I give you my blessing?"

I shrugged a major shrug, shoulders up around my ears. "I guess. I never really had this happen. Get a blessing. But sure."

The priest said, "Well, kneel."

So I knelt in front of this priest way out in the woods. He laid a hand on my forehead and gave me his blessing.

Then he knelt down in front of me and said, "Will you give me your blessing?"

I thought about it for a couple of seconds— then I gave him my blessing. I made it up on the spot. It must have been pretty good because tears came into his eyes.

Eventually I figured out that the Trappist monk's life might have been great for Thomas Merton but it wasn't for me. I haven't given anyone my blessing since that day in the woods behind Gethsemani. It was kind of cool, actually. I could be up for it again.

good morning, vietnam

MY TIME AT Vanderbilt came near the end of the Vietnam War, or at least what we thought might be the end. The draft lottery system was in effect and our best guess was that only the first fifty to sixty birth dates in the lottery would get drafted that year.

I'll never forget the night of the lottery. A lot of guys my age felt like vomiting all day. I went with some Vanderbilt friends to Ireland's, a popular bar near the school. The place was packed but it was quiet as a wake. We were all there to watch the lottery on television.

Yeah, it was on television. *Live.* A 1970s version of *The Hunger Games.* The TV announcer would call out a date—and a draft number. Like "January first, number three oh five."

All through that surreal night, there were loud groans and subdued sighs of relief around the bar. I'm not exaggerating that this was life-and-death stuff being decided.

My birthday came up. March 22.

I held my breath.

Then I got a draft number. It was two sixty-five. That meant that I probably wasn't going to Vietnam.

There was a catch — there's always a catch, right? This was my first year in grad school, and I could defer the draft, but for only one year. I had to leave Vanderbilt at the end of the school year, forfeiting the remainder of my three-year fellowship, or be thrown into next year's lottery.

That's the way the draft lottery worked. I could've returned to Vanderbilt in the fall and taken my chances that I'd get a high number in the next lottery. But that made me nervous. And honestly, after a year in the English literature PhD program, I knew I didn't want to teach creative writing or American lit in some college. I wanted to be a writer.

Interestingly, some journalists have reported that I "dropped out" of Vanderbilt. Not exactly. At best, misleading.

Actually, I dropped out of Vietnam.

master of english lit

SO THAT'S HOW I came to leave Vanderbilt University and give up my beautiful fellowship, my new Southern friends, my carrel in Kirkland Hall, and, most likely, my doctorate in English literature. For a while, the whole ordeal—the ridiculousness of it, the unfairness—put me in a dark mood.

I finally decided to at least get my master's degree. That was allowed under the rules.

My adviser in the English department encouraged me to write some fiction rather than a thesis on John Hawkes, which had been my original suggestion and a really bad idea. It may be hard to imagine that Hawkes—who wrote, "I began to write fiction on the assumption that the true enemies of the novel were plot, character, setting, and theme"—was once a hero of mine, but he was, back when I was a literary snoot.

God, was I pretentious and out of touch in those days. Nothing against John Hawkes, but I *love* plot, character, setting, and theme.

Anyway, I didn't have to go to Vietnam. Actually, I went into a different jungle.

mad men

i was in advertising—but i've been clean for over thirty years

HERE IS THE very first thing that happened to me in advertising.

On my *first* day, during the *first* hour—in the first *minute,* actually—I arrived at J. Walter Thompson New York's elevator bank and rushed to squeeze inside a closing door. Suddenly, I found myself staring at Arnold Grisman, the creative director who had hired me as a junior copywriter. I stopped for an instant. Just a beat. And the elevator door hit me in the head. Talk about starting with a bang.

Let's move on.

So, I found myself in advertising hell.

I should make it clear that I never chose a career in advertising. I didn't prepare for it, didn't take a single marketing or business course at Manhattan College or Vanderbilt University. I chose a career as a writer.

But when I arrived back in New York City from Nashville, I had no money. For around thirty-five dollars a week, I rented a room in the Washington Jefferson Hotel on West Fifty-First Street. The wallpaper in the room had a design with thousands and thousands of tiny pentagons. Picture this: Some past resident—psychotic or, at the very least, disturbingly obsessive—had penciled an *X* through every single pentagon. So I guess I got into advertising because I needed enough money to get the hell out of that creepy room in that seedy hotel and pay for groceries, electricity, and rent in pricey New York City.

My days passed like this:

I would write—by hand, in pencil—my novel early every morning, then report for duty at J. Walter Thompson, the world's largest advertising agency. I think it was the largest. Who really cares? (Note to copyeditor: Please don't look this up. Honestly, who cares?)

Here's what hell looked like: I worked in a very tightly constrained cubicle. The cubicle wall was maybe four and a half feet high. My work area had just enough room for me and a typewriter.

Now, *this* is why I remember the setup so vividly and why I knew it was the handiwork of Satan.

On the other side of the cubicle wall, about three feet from where I sat, was a water fountain. When people stopped by for a drink—every time anybody needed a gulp of water—their eyes would stare down at me while their mouths were moving. I had to decide whether to nod stupidly or smile stupidly or try to ignore them. It mostly depended on how loudly they were slurping.

This went on all day, every day, several times an hour, for my first year and a half at J. Walter Thompson. Satan's place of business.

My starting salary was six thousand dollars a year, which was less than peanuts, even back then.

Things got worse in a hurry. Nearly every week, Don Johnston, this skinny Connecticut Yankee who had risen from mail-room trainee to become Thompson's CEO, would call all of the employees down to the agency auditorium. *Not good, not good at all.*

Thompson's largest client was Ford, and Ford had a very bad story in those days. The car company's name had become a derogatory acronym. FORD stood for "Found on Road Dead" or "Fix or Repair Daily." At the first meeting I attended, CEO Johnston announced, "I regret to inform you we have lost the Ford Pinto and Ford Mustang accounts."

At this devastating news, advertising professionals, *adults,* started to cry. Leaving me to wonder if J. Walter Thompson was about to can me, and would that be such a bad thing?

The next week, an even skinnier Don Johnston was back at the microphone in the auditorium. "I regret to inform you we have lost the Singer Sewing Machine account."

A couple weeks later, Don Johnston was back again. "I regret to inform you that we have lost the RCA account." *Oh, c'mon, Donny, how about some good news. You're in advertising. Lie a little.*

So Thompson started firing people. As a new hire, I figured I would be one of the first to go. That's because I didn't understand how businesses are run. I was making so little working from my cubicle in hell, there was no point in getting rid of me.

Under normal circumstances, a junior copywriter at Thompson wouldn't get to smell a TV commercial, much less produce one. But suddenly, the most senior copywriters and pricey group heads were out on the street.

So I got television work.

The very first commercial I produced wound up being the highest-scoring automobile ad of the year. It was a split-screen spot comparing a Ford LTD and a Mercedes. I must've made the Ford LTD sound pretty damn good. That year, I went on to produce nine television commercials, which was a huge number even for a senior writer and unheard of for a junior.

Fix or Repair Daily loved me. Against my will, I began to get a reputation as a hot writer at Thompson, and my salary tripled from six thousand dollars to eighteen thousand. The crazy increase signaled they didn't want to lose me to another agency, but I had no intention of going anywhere. See, I wasn't really there—I wasn't an advertising copywriter, I was a novelist in the making. At least in my own mind.

One morning, the guy in charge of the Ford account deigned to stick his head into my cubicle. His pin-striped suit touched the walls of hell and got singed. He spoke. To me. "James, great to meet you. I've heard good things about you. Don Johnston knows who you are. I think you're the one who can solve a tough problem we're having on the Ford Torino business. You're going to be my guy on this. You'll report directly to me."

Hey, his little pep talk worked on me.

That held true until I heard his booming voice in the next cubicle. "Richie DiLallo, you're the man for this. Ford Torino's in trouble. You're the only one who can solve—"

life on the *way, way* upper west side

OKAY, OKAY, IT wasn't all bad. I was in my mid-twenties. I was living free and easy in the big city. I had a job that almost paid my bills.

There was a bodega across the street from my studio apartment on West One Hundredth and Manhattan Avenue. Nobody spoke much English in the bodega, and I knew very little Spanish, but all I could afford to buy and knew how to cook was bologna, bread, and beer. So it worked out okay. The people who owned the store were very nice. I think they took pity on me.

There was a jazz bar a couple of blocks away on Amsterdam Avenue. Almost everybody who went to the bar was Black. I obviously wasn't, but I got to be a regular. I was quiet, polite, and occasionally had a funny line for the bartender.

The place had live music every night. Late one evening, in comes the great Joe Cocker. He saunters up to the house band. They chat. They laugh. They chat some more. Then Joe plops down and plays the piano and sings for about two hours. "With a Little Help from My Friends" (the greatest cover ever), "Delta Lady." American blues. A lot of improvisational jazz.

It was unbelievable to be one of about thirty people in the room hearing this set. Almost un-real. I really needed to get home because I had ad hell in the morning, but I couldn't leave.

Best thing that happened to me since I'd worked at the Fillmore East.

the next raymond chandler?

WHEN I STARTED writing my first novel, *The Thomas Berryman Number,* I was still a literary twit. I'll prove it to you. The *Thomas* in the title was for lit darling Thomas McGuane, who published his first novel, *The Sporting Club,* just a year after completing a Stegner Fellowship at Stanford. *Berryman* was for John Berryman, the poet, who once gave a master class on fiction in a letter to his mother.

"The two great things are to be clear and short," Berryman wrote, "but rhythms matter too, and unexpectedness. You lead the reader briskly in one direction, then you spin him around, or you sing him a lullaby and then hit him on the head."

I was interested in sentences, not story, and definitely not in plot. I rationalized the writing of *The Thomas Berryman Number* by telling myself that mysteries could be considered legit fiction. Look at Raymond Chandler. Look at Dashiell Hammett.

Here's a quick story about Thomas McGuane—the *Thomas* in *Thomas Berryman*. When I was starting to write *The Thomas Berryman Number,* I sent a note to three of my favorite young writers just asking for advice. A kind word. Anything to buck up my courage.

McGuane was the only one who wrote back. He sent a postcard from Livingston, Montana. *Dear Jim… Write a good book. Your pal, Tom McGuane.*

I still have the postcard. And McGuane is still one of my favorite writers. How could he not be?

A year or so before I started *The Thomas Berryman Number,* I read *The Day of the Jackal* and *The Exorcist.* I liked both pacey, suspenseful, plot-heavy books *a lot.* So I kind of stopped being a full-bore literary snob. I didn't think I was capable of writing another *One Hundred Years of Solitude,* but I thought that *maybe* I could create something along the lines of *The Day of the Jackal.*

So every morning before work and every

night afterward, I typed out draft after draft of my mystery novel. I sat in a low metal chair pushed up to a kitchen counter that put my gloss-black Underwood Champion typewriter on a level with my chin.

Enough of that for now. I'll get into *Berryman* and publishing a little later in the story.

I will add this one little bit. After *The Thomas Berryman Number* was published—and made no money—I set out to write a big bestseller. I was dumb and arrogant enough to think that it would be easy. What half-decent writer couldn't churn out a cheesy bestseller? I made the same classic mistake that I see happen all the time in Hollywood: producers and studio executives try to duplicate a successful movie or TV show without really understanding *why* it worked.

Which is exactly what I set out to do. The new book was called *Season of the Machete*. I sent it to Ned Bradford, my brilliant editor at Little, Brown who had acquired *The Thomas Berryman Number*. He turned it down. As he should have, because the novel stunk. It was a derivative, incoherent hack job, and that's being kind.

Years later, when I actually had some idea of

what I was doing, I tried to rewrite *Season of the Machete*. I found the task hopeless. Stephen King once called me a terrible writer. I don't think that's true, but *Season of the Machete* was terrible, and I definitely wrote it.

my first, and last, autograph session

I NEVER GO to other writers' book signings, never have, not even when I was young and impressionable. Except for one rainy afternoon during my Mad Men days—before I'd actually published anything.

Newspaper columnist and novelist Jimmy Breslin was appearing at the Barnes & Noble on Fifth Avenue, not far from J. Walter Thompson's offices in the Graybar Building on Lexington Avenue. I loved Breslin's writing, his very New York, very Queens voice. So I braved the monsoon raging outside and went to see if maybe whatever he had was contagious.

While Breslin was signing his new book for me, I mumbled something like "I just finished a first novel."

Breslin didn't even bother to look up. He said, "Yeah, so?"

Yeah, so?

I don't think he was trying to be funny, but maybe he was. I mean, the line *could* have been very funny. At the time, I thought, *Oh, man, thanks a lot, Breslin, you fuck.*

I figured he wasn't really a bad person, but... what a prick.

Or, hell, maybe he *was* just very funny. I mean, I know he was funny—as a writer, anyway. He'd proven that with *The Gang That Couldn't Shoot Straight.*

So when I sign books for people, I'm really kind. Always. I learned that from Jimmy Breslin.

a penthouse with no kitchen

MY COOKIE-CUTTER studio apartment on One Hundredth Street across from the bodega was starting to wear on me. So every Sunday I'd first scan, then very closely read, the *New York Times* listings for apartment rentals. As soon as the big, fat paper hit the newsstand, I'd buy a copy.

Then, early that morning, I'd start making house calls.

One snowy Sunday I found a listing for a "penthouse studio" on Riverside Drive. It was on the southwest corner of a gorgeous twenty-two-story prewar building overlooking a small park and the river. The rent was $225 a month. I rushed over to see this mini-penthouse that sounded way too good to be true. Minutes after I got there, two other potential tenants arrived. This was going to be a New York, New

York, shoot-out and it was probably going to get ugly in a hurry.

The agent, a very fair-minded woman, said to me, "James, you were here first. But you've got to decide now."

So here's the catch with the penthouse studio. It had a wraparound terrace. It had a great view up and down the Hudson River. But there was no kitchen. And to get out on the terrace, you had to climb onto the toilet seat and go through a narrow bathroom window.

No problem that I could see.

I told the agent, "I'll take it!"

My new studio had once been the master bedroom in the model Lauren Hutton's apartment. It had windows facing the southwest, and the wall opposite those windows was all mirrors. When the sun was setting, the light was blinding. Seriously, coming from outside and opening the front door could give you a headache and make your eyes bleed. The sun coming down over the river was enough in itself, but then it hit all six mirror panes, so you had six reflected suns, plus the real sun. It was insane. I loved it! What a place to write and do other things.

Singer-songwriter Laura Nyro lived in the

apartment next door. Laura had been only nine-teen when she released her debut album, and she'd written a lot of famous songs since, like "Gonna Take a Miracle" and "Midnight Blue."

Laura was nice to me, the almost perfect neighbor—except that a couple of nights a week, she would go out on her terrace, which connected to my terrace, to compose and sing songs. Sometimes she sang with a couple of friends—in particular, the one and only Patti LaBelle. Laura and Patti would conduct songfests at midnight, at one in the morning, at two in the morning. On the one hand, I'm thinking, *This is very cool.* On the other...*In a couple hours, I've got to go to work.* Much more important, before I went to work, I had to write some more pages of *The Thomas Berryman Number.*

the last of "moon river"

MOST OF THE pretty good things that happened during my early years in New York didn't have much to do with advertising. In those days, J. Walter had a specialty group called Communispond that taught businesspeople how to speak coherently and persuasively in public. It also taught Thompson folk how to sell better ads, or even not-so-good ads.

Communispond was a two-person operation. The guy who ran it was a total crazy man named Jim McGurk. McGurk's most recent job before arriving at Communispond had been managing Monti Rock III in Vegas. Monti Rock, if you don't know, was a comedian-singer who was born Joseph Montanez Jr. He used to be a regular guest on *The Tonight Show* with Johnny Carson. Carson loved Monti, who'd had a couple of disco hit records—"Get Dancin'" and "I Wanna Dance wit' Choo"—and a credited cameo in *Saturday Night Fever* but basically was just a very funny character.

Jim McGurk had gotten Monti a yearlong gig at Caesars Palace on the Vegas Strip. It was a huge deal for both of them. But Monti was certifiably nuts. His cabaret act in Vegas required nine costume changes. After a week of shows, he pleaded with McGurk: "I can't go on doing this, Jimmy. I can't do it, Jimmy. Jimmy, I can't do this. Jimmy, help me. Jimmy, please save me."

So, in the show's second week, after the seventh or eighth costume change, Monti gave up and came out stark-raving drunk, then fell off the stage. What happens in Vegas stays in Vegas, right? Well, obviously *not,* since I'm telling you the story.

The next thing McGurk knows, he and Monti are practically run out of Vegas—and McGurk finds himself supervising a two-person training division at J. Walter Thompson, which he called "J. Walter Tombstone."

McGurk and I became friendly. We'd go out drinking a couple times a week. Then one night he invited me to go with him to see Monti Rock's apartment. "Like, tonight? Really? Okay. Sure." But *why?*

What a lovely madhouse it turned out to be. Larger-than-life Greek and Roman statuary everywhere. Lots and lots of variously shaped and sized penises. Strange oil portraits of very unusual-looking men and maybe a few women. It was kind of hard to tell.

And Monti. I was invited to sit on a ruby-red velvet couch next to him.

Monti leans in and says in a whispery voice, "James, I just recorded two very beautiful songs for my new album. Would you like to hear them? It would be an honor for me to sing for you."

I look over at McGurk, who shrugs and nods. So what can I say? "That'd be an honor for me too."

The next thing I know, Monti Rock III turns on this recording of himself singing "Moon River." He's sitting about a foot away from me on the couch and he's singing along with the record. He's singing right in my ear.

"Moon River" was never the same for me after that.

making thirty-second movies

THE BEST THING about writing TV commercials is that eventually the creative team has to go film them on location. Depending on the budget and client, you maybe stay at quaint little places like the Beverly Hills Hotel and Shutters in LA and Brown's in London.

Early on, one of the funnier veteran creatives at J. Walter Thompson New York gave me the insider pro's secret to writing for TV. "You need to write every script like this: 'Open on powerful surf in Hawaii—cut to toilet being flushed.'" The key was to make sure the Hawaii scene was *in the script.* That way they would send you to Hawaii to film the surf. At least, that's how it worked back in the Mad Men days.

At that time, Jess Corman was the king of radio at Thompson. One day, I was given some radio work and had to go meet him for the first time. I walked into a corner office and found a long-haired older dude along with two young copywriters—Mitch Silver, who eventually wrote a couple of novels, and Richard DiLallo, whose name you might recognize from some of our collaborations.

I looked at the older guy and asked, "Are you Jess Corman?"

And he came right back with "Why? Does he owe you money?"

I started laughing, and ever since, whenever someone asks me, "Are you James Patterson?," I've been using that line: "Why? Does he owe you money?"

Anyway, I enjoyed going on film shoots—usually to exotic locales like Bismarck, North Dakota, and Flower Mound, Texas—but my absolute favorite thing about advertising was the music sessions. We would get some of the best talent in New York. Sometimes a violin section would arrive in the studio straight from Lincoln Center to do a ridiculous ten seconds in a thirty-second jingle. Tina Turner occasionally recorded commercial tracks. Nick Ashford and Valerie Simpson were married songwriting partners. As Ashford and Simpson, they wrote "Ain't No Mountain High Enough" (inspired by the tall buildings Nick noticed as he walked along Central Park West when he was a struggling young performer) and "I'm Every Woman." They loved to work and were always fun to be around. So was Barry Manilow. When Michael Bolton was singing on a session (he sang on some Kodak tracks for me, courtesy of my music-producer friend Susan Hamilton), a lot of women from Thompson, and some men, would show up just to watch.

Not just listen—*watch*.

one night in chicago

I WAS TWENTY-SIX or twenty-seven, still working out of a cubicle in New York. Burt Manning, who had been creative director in the Chicago office, was transferred to New York to fix the place, which was a sinking ship at the time. Or maybe the ship had already sunk and nobody bothered to notice.

Almost immediately, Burt became my mentor. Why? Because I chopped wood—I worked hard—and I could write. I could also write fast.

Of course, Burt was a mentor who could torture you. He browbeat the hell out of me on a daily basis. I really didn't like writing ads, but he made me aware of the importance of every sentence, the importance of one sentence flowing into the next, and how you had to always remember you were talking to an audience—and that audience had absolutely no interest in what you had to say about beer, beans, or beauty cream.

Advertising is usually created by pairs or teams of art directors and writers. Burt liked to work lean, and that's what I learned to do too. I was my own staff. I worked alone, didn't even have an art director. The arrangement has served me well.

Within a few months, Burt put me in charge of the Quaker business, which he'd brought with him to New York. The food conglomerate Quaker was his safety net, his leverage. It was a lot of billing for a soft-spoken, small-town kid like me to be handling.

Three days a week I had to work out of Thompson Chicago in the John Hancock building, where they set me up in a big office with multiple picture windows overlooking Lake Michigan. I also got to stay in a two-bedroom suite in the Hampshire House off Michigan Avenue. Everybody in the Chicago office thought I was Burt's boy, some big-deal writer coming out there from New York. But I was just this naive kid rescued from a cubicle next to the water fountain.

One of the Thompson account executives

on the Quaker business helped me settle into Chicago. The exec lived out in the suburbs, a forty- to forty-five-minute commute. He and I had to be in an early meeting—7:15—at Quaker's corporate headquarters in the Merchandise Mart. So he asked if he could crash in my suite at the Hampshire House.

The two of us had dinner at Eli's the Place for Steak, then we headed back to the hotel. Around eleven, I got into bed. Five minutes later the door to my bedroom creaked open.

Without saying a word to me, the account executive jumped into my bed. He wasn't wearing anything.

Now, understand that I worked for this man. Also, this was 1974. I couldn't believe what was happening. I tried to handle it as well as I could. "I don't know where you picked up this idea. This isn't going to happen. You have to get out of my bed. You have to go. Please leave."

The account executive finally got out of the bed and he left. He didn't say a word to me that night. He didn't talk about it the following morning either. Like it never happened.

The incident shook me up. I was never physically threatened, but I felt betrayed. And hurt. Obviously, I never forgot it. It's the kind of situation that in this day would have been a big issue inside any company.

Maybe I should have, but I didn't bring it to Human Resources. I think I didn't want to talk about it to anybody. It was a different time.

newburgh on my mind

JAMES TAYLOR HAD Carolina on his mind. I had upstate New York. While I was working at Thompson, I got a call from a New York state trooper who said he was phoning from my grandmother's house in Newburgh. I immediately thought, *Oh, Jesus, Nan passed.*

The trooper asked if I was James Patterson. When I said yes, he explained that my grandmother had reported a missing person. My grandfather. Pop was MIA.

"I'll be there as soon as I can," I told the trooper. I rented a car and sped up the thruway to my old hometown, a trip that always gave me the willies.

I arrived at Nan's house and it was like old times. She made hot tea with milk, cut me a piece of homemade babka, and we talked things out. Finally, I said, "Let's go for a ride."

Nan was always game for a car ride. She and Pop had gone on car rides every Sunday since I'd been little.

I drove Nan to Calvary Cemetery in Newburgh. We got out of the car and took a walk. I showed her Pop's grave.

All Nan said was "Oh, yeah."

She was a funny lady. She started laughing when she realized that she'd forgotten that Pop had been dead for ten years. We held hands and said a little prayer for him. I said a prayer for Pop's neighbor and for my first-kiss girl, Veronica Tabasco. Then we went home.

Nan wasn't just funny, though; she was a pretty cool lady in all ways. She was a really good storyteller with a quick wit and fire in her eyes. In my head, right now, my grandmother is one hundred fourteen. The way I like to look at it, she's still alive as long as I'm around to tell her stories.

the best ad line i ever wrote

IT'S THE REALLY funny, totally unexpected lines in the ad game that you remember. Most of the time they're satiric lines that never get close to being presented to a client. Before he became a restaurateur on Long Island, Jerry Della Femina wrote this theme line for Panasonic: "From those wonderful folks who gave you Pearl Harbor." I know that one didn't get to the client, but it became the attention-grabbing title for Della Femina's autobiography.

So Thompson Chicago was going after the Schlitz beer account. In those days, Schlitz was seen — at least by the people at Schlitz — as a premium lager. My own taste buds didn't happen to agree. I thought Schlitz was a below-average American lager. And that's how I came to write my favorite advertising line.

"Schlitz Shitz."

Truth in advertising, right?

Of course, we never brought that slogan out to the client. Schlitz went with the line "Go for it." I still think "Schlitz Shitz" is better. It's definitely memorable.

Full disclosure. I did write quite a few ad lines that saw the light of day. "Aren't you hungry for Burger King?" Kodak: "Picture a brand-new world." The best-known slogan would probably be "I'm a Toys 'R' Us Kid." Oh, yeah, I renamed Allegheny Airlines (better known at the time as Agony Airlines) US Air. And that's more than enough about ad slogans.

when you're going through hell—just keep going

SOMETIMES I'M ASKED how I know so much about serial killers. I say, "I met a few when I was in advertising." Some were Thompson clients. One particularly odious marketing guy at Burger King, one from Nestlé, and several from Unilever come to mind and still give me the occasional nightmare.

Meanwhile, the advertising crazies just kept coming at me. I started working for a fascinating character by the name of Frank Nicolo. Frank had come from a small agency where he'd been very successful, a real advertising star. He introduced French-based Club Méditerranée (Club Med) to the U.S. with the line "Spend one week half clad, flat broke, and happy about it." He did smart London Fog ads, like the one that showed a man next to a Salvation Army box saying, "So long, old friend," as he reluctantly parted with his well-worn London Fog raincoat.

Frank was very, very good, but he was also a mad scientist—the genius kind. He was an incredible workaholic while somehow also being a sweetheart, an Italian mensch. People who worked for him wandered around muttering things like "Weekends are made for Nicolo" (a play on the old Michelob beer line "Weekends are made for Michelob"). And my personal Nicolo favorite: "If you don't come in on Saturday, don't bother to come in on Sunday."

One evening, late, Burt Manning came to see me and Nicolo.

He reiterated the conditions that had been in place since I was hired in '71. Thompson New York was trapped in a decade-long tailspin. The creative work was bad. The clients were mostly difficult to work for (except the Kodak people, who were great). Morale was terrible.

Burt told us the New York office couldn't afford to lose any more accounts. In private, he'd already explained Nicolo's Mad Men methodology to me. "Frank will get to creative solutions most people won't even think of, because he's so obsessive. You'll think you have the answer and Frank will keep pushing, pushing, pushing.

He's going to drive you crazy, but I think it will be worth it. You'll come out of this as a better writer. Or you'll wind up back at that madhouse you worked in as a college kid. Only now you'll be a patient."

Anyway, a new bank client was the New York office's latest hot potato. Frank and I were given the account and told to save it at any cost to our mental or physical health. The hyperactive marketing guy who ran the bank's business wasn't a bad human being, but he was yet another total madman in my life.

All through the normal workday, every day, he would call us half a dozen times. Finally, Nicolo came up with an idea that only he could've thought of. He explained to me that the only way to beat this client was to out-crazy him.

So we started inviting the bank's marketing guy into the office to join our day-and-night-long work sessions on his business. One afternoon around four days in, he actually fell asleep at Frank's desk. That was the end of it. Our madman was better than the bank's madman.

Like Frank Nicolo, Burt Manning worked seven days a week, twenty hours a day at times. The man never slept. I can remember waiting outside his office at nine o'clock on a Saturday night. He had a lineup of six creative teams waiting to see him. And just because you were the first in line didn't mean anything. You waited until he said it was your turn.

I'll tell you what, though. To Burt's credit, he went on to completely turn J. Walter Thompson's fortune around and restore it to its former glory—not only in New York, but all over the world.

Every day working for Burt was a little harrowing. But he taught me a lot. Burt liked to say, "I taught Jim everything he knows. Just not everything I know."

I watch ads these days and I usually think, *They need Burt Manning*. The man could turn a phrase.

when insanity feels like sanity

I'VE MADE NINE holes in one—I swear to God—but I've never come close to figuring out the game of golf. The only thing I remember from the couple of lessons I took from master teacher Jim McLean was him telling me, "You're not good enough to shoot for pins"—flagsticks. "Just aim for the middle of the green." Hurtful. But sound advice. Saved me from losing a lot of balls.

Anyway, golf supplied some much-needed sanity in my life during the Mad Men years. Well, not exactly sanity. Just a different kind of insanity.

Frank Nicolo was my partner for some ultra-crazy golf escapades. At least once a week, after work at the agency, we'd drive out to City Island and whack a hundred or so golf balls on a very dark, very cold golf range stuck in the middle of nowhere.

Just so you get the picture, I'm talking about smacking half-dead balls in the dead of winter—ten, twenty degrees, cold wind a-blowing, no heaters at this godforsaken range.

Our attitude was that if it was a winter day when we wouldn't mind taking a long walk, the golf game was on. Here's how desperate we were to play. One winter Saturday we drove to a crummy public course in South Jersey. It was so cold you couldn't hammer a tee into the ground. The golf course was also overrun by geese. So we started teeing up our balls on a couple of frozen goose turds.

One other time, Nicolo and I played a round of golf on December 24.

This particular day before Christmas, it started snowing when we were on the third green. We kept playing and it kept getting more absurd.

The ball wouldn't roll on the fairways. You couldn't putt because the ball would gather snow and stop halfway to the hole.

So we quit after we finished nine holes. We were actually proud of ourselves for quitting. That might have been a first for us. As we were heading to the clubhouse, four die-hard New Yorkers came walking through the driving snow in the direction of the first tee. We over-heard one guy say, "So, Marty, you think we'll get in eighteen holes?"

Probably some ad guys, like us. Or maybe Mafia hitmen taking a little time off for Christmas.

Another time, Nicolo and I—plus our sports-journalist pal Johnny Keresty—played with another friend who was in his mid-seventies, a very good golfer named Charlie Malone from the great Commonwealth of Massachusetts.

We were playing one of the ten thousand or so courses around Myrtle Beach, South Carolina. Frank, Keresty, and I hit half a dozen balls into the water on a fairly easy par-three hole. In our defense, we had just taken up the game.

Charlie Malone stepped up to his ball, waggled his club thrice, then looked over at us. "Tough hole, hey, boys?" He grinned and put his tee shot about five feet from the hole.

Yet another good reason to quit golf.

But to this day, I persist. The golf gods are diabolically clever. They know how to keep you coming back.

Much like the writing gods.

the hamburger wars

J. WALTER THOMPSON very aggressively went
after the massive Burger King account one year.
Burt Manning led the charge. I'll spare you the
gory details, but we won the business—which
was always invigorating until we remembered,
*Now we actually have to do the work and deliver
on our ridiculous promises.*

The fast-food company was a Pillsbury sub-
sidiary and the billing was almost as large as
the rest of the New York office's put together.
Frank Nicolo was picked to run creative on the
account. I supervised the adult business, while
wordsmith Hal Friedman and a very bright
writer named Linda Kaplan were in charge of
Burger King's large kids' program. (Linda went
on to start her own billion-dollar ad agency.
Good for Linda. She's one of my heroes.)

It was Nicolo who must take most of the

blame for creating the very creepy Magic Burger King, a red-bearded Tudor-costumed character who, for a brief shining moment, became more popular than Ronald McDonald. That was probably a mistake on our part. We were starting to get under Old McDonald's skin. More on that soon.

"Aren't you hungry for Burger King now?" was a campaign that I created. My bad. I called this style of advertising "hard sell that people love to watch." I know, it makes no sense. But clients seemed to buy it.

The Battle of the Burgers was also one of my creations. In those ads, many of which were penned by Friedman, Burger King got aggressive with Old McDonald's. Burger King broiled its meat; Old McDonald's fried theirs. Burger King's regular hamburger was bigger than Old McDonald's regular hamburger. Most of the spots were charming and funny, which they needed to be. We were going up against an American icon, a very rich and powerful icon.

For some reason, the whole country took note of these ads. Almost every night, the campaign was featured on the TV evening news. Dan Rather would comment on the latest ads in "the Burger Wars." He'd show one of our TV spots as part of the newscast. It was even better than free advertising. The story was covered in newspapers and magazines like *Time* and *Newsweek*. Of course, this was back in the day when some people actually watched the nightly news on TV and read newspapers and magazines made of paper.

Maybe it was the baseball-themed spots that ran during the Cardinals versus Brewers World Series, but the loftier-than-thou McDonald's Corporation got so irritated, they filed a lawsuit in federal court. All of the suspect Thompsonites were deposed, but nothing much came of the claims against the taste-test research. I couldn't help feeling that the whole thing was unnecessary and kind of hilarious. The Battle of the Burgers! C'mon. But I loved goosing Old McDonald's. To be fair, I enjoy an occasional Quarter Pounder, and I'm a fan of Ronald McDonald House and all the good it does.

Meanwhile, I continued to work on my novels. I'd write early in the morning, every morning. I'd lock my office door at lunchtime and write for half an hour. I'd write on the plane during every business trip. I'd write pages at four in the morning, and I'd write again until midnight. I refused to give up on myself. Though maybe I should have. I finished *See How They Run* and *Black Friday,* and both novels were pretty bad. Then I wrote *The Midnight Club,* which I thought was decent. I hoped I was finally learning from my mistakes.

Then one day I came up with a character I really liked—she was called Alexis Cross. That's right; when I started writing *Along Came a Spider,* Alex was a woman.

But I'm getting ahead of myself again. My brain works a lot faster than my pencil.

the hellfires get even hotter

I CAN DESCRIBE my success in advertising, and even in publishing, in one off-color paragraph.

When I was the young creative director at Thompson New York, a crafty veteran account man by the name of Bob Norsworthy thought that I was arrogant and full of crap. He wasn't all wrong. But I kept making the right decisions. And so Norsworthy—a very funny raconteur from Kentucky—came up with the following: "If Jim Patterson says a grasshopper can pull a plow, hitch up that little motherfucker."

What Bob Norsworthy meant, I think, was that I had a good gut, good instincts for what was going to work and what wasn't. *Is it that simple?* Sometimes, I think that it is.

Meanwhile, Advertising Satan continued to use his wiles on me. I was in my mid-thirties when I became the youngest creative director ever at J. Walter New York. Or so they told me.

I was always clear about the work—what was good, what wasn't. I would always say, "This is just my opinion"—but in the end, I was the person in charge. I didn't often take the praise, but I always took the blame.

Around this time, I teamed up with Steve Bowen, an ex-Marine who used to keep a grenade on his desk. I don't think it was an armed grenade, but it sure looked like it. And he thought it made his point, whatever in hell his point was.

That was Steve's style: macho and Marine, provocative, combative, and, occasionally, a little hard to understand.

Steve had a way of speaking that people in the office came to call "Bowenisms." He did come out with some unforgettable lines. "There's got to be a golden pony somewhere in all this horse shit" and "You can't leap tall buildings with a puckered asshole." Steve Bowen might have been a distant cousin of my old high-school principal, Brother Leonard.

He was a great partner for me. I tended to be more measured. Somehow our partnership worked oddly well. When he and I took the reins at Thompson New York, the flagship office was seen as stodgy, old J. Walter. We pulled off some loony-tunes-crazy stunts to try and counter the image.

J. Walter Thompson had moved its offices a few blocks north. One night, we commandeered the lobby at 466 Lexington and threw a totally ridiculous WrestleMania event. At least we understood how absurd it was. I did, anyway. Steve—not so much. We invited the entire New York advertising community to come to dowdy J. Walter Thompson to watch live wrestling in the enormous atrium at 466, have some laughs, and party like it was 1999, a decade or so in the future. Most of the agencies came, and they partied, and Thompson's image changed almost overnight.

When Steve and I took over the New York office, our largest account was health-care and consumer-products giant Warner-Lambert. Less than a week into the job, we were summoned to meet with their COO and president, Mel Goodes. We knew it wasn't going to be a fun visit to Morris Plains, New Jersey.

Mel turned out to be a good guy, but at that first meeting he told us, "Look, fellas, right now we've got three ad agencies—Thompson,

Y and R, and Ted Bates. I'm sorry to say this, but I have to rank you guys *fourth* out of three."

I told Steve I thought I could not only fix the problem but that I could fix it almost overnight. But it would take some courage from the account managers—the Suits. Steve was on my side, and he was never lacking for courage. The few, the proud, the ex-Marines.

In recent years Thompson had been bringing Warner-Lambert as many as a dozen creative approaches for every assignment, then letting them pick. The Suits were responsible for that strategy. In my opinion, it was suicidal. No agency could create a dozen approaches that had any chance of working in the marketplace. From that day on, we presented only two or three campaigns, and only ones we believed in. Steve and I promised each Warner-Lambert brand manager that we knew the difference. They began to trust us.

Within a year, Mel Goodes invited Steve and me to dinner at the Palm and said we were now his number 1. He picked up the check for dinner (a rarity for clients) and also handed us a bundle of new business.

During the next four years, Bowen and I

doubled the size of the New York office—*twice*. I hated to admit it, but advertising hell was almost starting to be fun. I was beginning to enjoy the constant fires and the blistering heat.

The New York office was thriving. But Thompson was having big troubles elsewhere. Industry analyst Alan J. Gottesman quipped that J. Walter Thompson "[has] problems in places where other companies don't even have places."

hitch up that little grasshopper

ONE BIG PROBLEM with the creative department at J. Walter Thompson was that—when I started running it, at least—nobody very good wanted to work there. I doubted that we could recruit a decent porter. Thompson New York was seen as uptight, stodgy, and not very creative.

How uptight? Back when I was hired, female vice presidents were encouraged to wear hats inside the office, and women weren't allowed in the executive dining room; instead, waiters in tuxes brought lunch to their offices on trays under silver plate covers. Fortunately, most of that had changed by the time I became creative director, but we still had a ways to go.

Necessity truly is the mother of invention, so here's what I decided to do about our personnel problems in the 1980s. I ran a full-page ad in the *New York Times*. Back page of the business section.

The headline got right to the point: "Write If You Want Work."

What followed in the ad was a test for writers and other creatives. Eight deceptively tricky questions. Here are four of them:

The ingredients listed on the tin of baked beans read: "Beans, Water, Tomatoes, Sugar, Salt, Modified Starch, Vinegar, Spices." Make it sound mouthwatering.

You may have heard this story about the person who made a fortune selling refrigerators to Eskimos. In not more than 100 words, how would you sell a telephone to a Trappist monk who is observing the strict Rule of Silence? (But the monk can nod acceptance at the end.)

Design/draw two posters. One is for legislating strict gun control laws. The other is in support of the NRA.

You just learned that the IRS is planning to lower the percentage ratio of income to medical expenses, thus lowering the tax deductions for dental, psychiatric, and medical expenses. You are a reporter for a daily newspaper. The editor wants to make this a banner story. Write a compelling headline in a coherent two-column story.

The reason I ran the ad was that I was desperate, but I also suspected there were talented people out there who would be great in advertising—they just didn't know how to get in the front door.

So I made it easy for them. I showed them a side door.

We received a couple thousand submissions and we hired eight writers from that one ad in the *New York Times*. We then sent the ad and the story around to the media, who proceeded to run our ad *for free*.

Over the next few years, we hired over fifty writers based on "Write If You Want Work" and a couple of interviews. I could evaluate the test-takers in a couple of minutes and immediately tell (a) whether they could write worth a damn, and (b) whether they could solve problems.

Of the fifty-plus creatives we eventually hired, only one didn't work out, and that was because he was claustrophobic and couldn't be in an office.

My favorite hire turned out to be my eventual kids' book partner and pal Chris Grabenstein.

Another good hire, Dan Staley, went on to become a producer on *Cheers*. Tony Puryear wrote the original screenplay for the hit movie *Eraser*. Craig Gillespie directed *I, Tonya*.

Good for all of them.

life after miller high life

THE BEST AND the worst thing about advertising hell was the New Business Pitch. It was winner-take-all. May the best bullshitters win. And these one- to two-hour take-no-prisoners shoot-outs cost a fortune, all of it out of pocket for the agency.

Thompson got invited to pitch for the Miller High Life beer account. Miller was owned by Philip Morris and they were spending ninety million dollars a year, which was a lot of money back then. Maybe it still is. I've lost track and I've lost interest.

The pitch was a big deal at Thompson, of course, but CEO Burt Manning and new business director Bert Metter had a sometime tendency to overdo things. We'd already had four grueling rehearsals by the time we flew out to Milwaukee. What was worse, Burt and

Bert insisted that we meet that night at Miller headquarters around ten and practice the pitch all over again.

When the creative team—Hal Friedman, Brian Sitts, Frank Nicolo, and myself—got into Milwaukee, I made the command decision that we were not going to meet Burt and Bert at Miller headquarters. We were going out for steaks and beer.

The next morning, we showed up for the big presentation around seven thirty. In those days, Miller actually had beer taps in the lobby. Maybe they still do. Frank Nicolo drew himself a beer, took a healthy swig, and said it was good for client relations.

When we got up to the conference room, Burt and Bert wouldn't talk to us before the pitch. They were really pissed. I got it. My team and I had blown them off the night before.

When the pitch was over—a really good pitch—Burt and Bert still wouldn't talk to us.

But two days later, when we got the news that we'd won the Miller account, Burt and Bert immediately started talking to us again. They even popped some champagne down in Burt's office. And Burt could really heap on the praise when it was earned.

Not long after we won Miller, we had to go to Philip Morris headquarters to meet with Hamish Maxwell, who ran the corporation. I'll never forget entering the Philip Morris board-room and seeing a pack of cigarettes placed at every chair around the big table. How frick-ing bizarre is that? Or maybe not, given that Maxwell was a two-pack-a-day smoker.

During the meeting, Hamish Maxwell said a line that's stuck with me: "I've been bamboo-zled before, but now I've been bamboozled by the best."

Now, here's the strangest part of all. Years later, I had to take a little heart exam at New York–Presbyterian Hospital. So I go up to the fourth floor, start walking to the front desk, and stop dead in my tracks. Big letters spell out HAMISH MAXWELL PAVILION.

Think about it. I definitely did. The man, since deceased, who had been the chairman of Philip Morris, makers of Marlboro, Virginia Slims, Chesterfield, and Player's cigarettes, now had his name emblazoned over the front desk of the clinic where my heart was about to be examined.

I had to stop myself from running the hell out of there. But I stayed. They're very good at what they do in the Hamish Maxwell Pavilion.

I'm fine, by the way.

Maybe because I didn't drink any beer at Miller headquarters.

Or maybe because I didn't smoke the cigarettes at Philip Morris headquarters, or anywhere else.

the fine art of negotiating

IN 1987, BRITISH marketing group WPP swooped in like a horde of Harpies to buy J. Walter. Don Johnston was still chairman and CEO. He'd put on a couple of pounds, thank God. Threatened by WPP's tiny titan Martin Sorrell—who by purchasing competitors had expanded the company, originally named Wire and Plastic Products, from shopping-basket maker to branding powerhouse—Johnston was concerned about retaining key clients and key personnel. So Thompson offered me three lucrative financial packages to choose from.

I had at the time a very creative financial adviser, Lloyd Zeiderman. Among Zeiderman's clients were a young Tom Cruise, Superman (aka Christopher Reeve), and country singer Kenny Rogers. Lloyd taught me a secret of successful negotiating that I never forgot.

I sent the three financial packages over to Lloyd's office and asked for his thoughts and a recommendation. That same afternoon, he told me to pop over and we'd chat and come up with a cool plan to conquer the world. That's how Lloyd talked. We would "chat," it would be "cool," and we would "conquer the world."

I was definitely curious about which of the three packages Lloyd felt was best for me.

His advice blew me away. "Jim, this is a fuckin' no-brainer. You take *all three packages*. If they put it on the table, they're willing to give it to you. Don't ever leave anything on the table. We cool?"

So that's what I did and pretty much what I got from Thompson. And I never forgot that lesson about negotiating. It probably raised WPP's Martin Sorrell's blood pressure a couple of notches. I liked that a lot. I always thought of Sir Martin as a somewhat witty accountant, a rather unpleasant, fire-breathing bean counter. I never gave on a single point from that negotiation.

But the shining star of my investment life, the one who has kept me safe and sane, who's helped me sleep nights, is Tony Peyser.

I remember back in 2008, Tony and I were talking about what a terrible year it had been. We did a whole lot better than most, but the very best thing Tony did was keep Bernie Madoff away from my door. Madoff had come calling, but he wouldn't explain how he was delivering his attractive dividends year after year. So Tony sent him packing.

He's also gotten me out of a bad business deal, helped me buy houses and cars, drawn up about a thousand assorted contracts for me.

I still sleep well, and I'm going to sleep well tonight, because of Tony Peyser.

life lessons

I HAD NEVER thought of myself as a true Mad Man, but for the next couple of years I got obsessive about advertising. To my surprise, maybe even shock, I quickly rose to become CEO of Thompson North America. I was still in my thirties. On the side, I was writing one or two bestselling novels a year. It was nuts. Something had to give or eventually I would.

Life lessons are everywhere, right? The trouble is, like most people, I tended to ignore them. I soldiered on through long days and nights. I was working too hard. I knew it.

But every once in a while, I snapped out of it and actually paid attention.

It happened to me on the New Jersey Turnpike, of all unlikely places. One Sunday afternoon, I had to leave the Jersey Shore for a meeting in New York. The last thing that I wanted to do was schlep back to work. The last place I wanted to be was hot, sweaty New York City in July.

An hour and a half after I left the shore, I was still trapped in bumper-to-bumper traffic. The proverbial turnpike parking lot. Cars moving at ten miles an hour.

On the other side of the road, an occasional car went whizzing by. *Whoosh*. Maybe one car every fifteen seconds.

Whoosh...

Whoosh...

Whoosh...

I sat there, mildly pissed, absorbing this very obvious life lesson for about an hour.

Then I finally got it. The lesson was simple and so very clear. Why hadn't I seen it before?

My mission in life had to be to get on the other side of the highway. To get in the traffic lane that was moving. My life was going in the wrong direction.

I swear to God, that insight, that miserable time trapped on the Jersey Turnpike, drove me out of advertising.

I focused on writing novels.

And I made it my mission to try and find somebody who would love me and who I would love back.

Whoosh . . . whoosh.

escape from new york

ONE EVENING, A week or so after my epiphany in New Jersey, Burt Manning invited me to dinner at 21 Club, one of his favorite eating spots in New York. It was always a treat for me to break bread with Burt. He's an interesting guy—a talented conversationalist and a good listener. That's a rare combination. He's also a winner. He literally saved Thompson. Burt wanted to talk about my future, and he told me I could be as big as I wanted to be in the ad world.

At this point, around 1996, I'd written four bestselling novels featuring Alex Cross. I'd also had that epiphany on the Jersey Turnpike. So I told Burt I didn't have a future in advertising. I don't actually remember this, but Burt later told me I said, "Burt, I can't afford to work at Thompson anymore."

I guess the kid from the country had finally come of age. I believed I was ready to be a full-time writer.

After I formally quit, I stayed on the J. Walter Thompson board of directors for a couple of years. It's interesting that when you leave a job, but you're still technically there, you're not really there. I wasn't, anyway. Not in mind, and not in spirit. It started to get a little ridiculous.

I can still remember sitting in the Thompson boardroom and feeling trapped. I'd look at my watch and think, *Oooh, it's only 8:30…*

I'd catch myself looking at my watch again. *Oooh, it's only 8:51…*

Oooh, 9:14.

Oooh, 9:31.

And that is precisely why I've refused to sit on any boards since I left Thompson. For me, life is too short for board meetings.

But let me tell you, life is pretty good for a bestselling writer. I think maybe I was born for this. And I still look at the world through the lens of a kid from Newburgh, New York. That helps me stay down-to-earth. Keeps things real, keeps me humble.

i guess i'm a writer now

passion keeps you going ... but it doesn't pay the rent

WHEN I FIRST arrived in New York, I would force myself to get up at five every morning to squeeze in a couple of hours of writing before I went to work at the ad factory. I was full of hope and big dreams but not enough confidence to quit my day job and write for my supper.

I'd play some music, maybe a little Harry Nilsson ("Gotta Get Up"), and do my first stint of scribbling sentences, cutting sentences, adding sentences, driving myself crazy.

The book's getting better, right?

The book's getting worse. Every sentence I write is inferior to the last.

I'm going to be the next Graham Greene.

Don't quit your day job, chump.

You start thinking you're a fraud, "a big fat failure." Okay, okay, so that's a line out of the movie *You've Got Mail.* So is "You are what you read."

As I said, I was driving myself crazy. It goes with the territory. I think that's what first-time novelists are supposed to do. Our rite of passage. Every night after work, I'd come home in a daze of jingle lyrics and cutesy catch-phrases, sit in my kitchen, stare around at the tiny antiseptic space, then start writing again. I'd go till eleven or twelve. That's how I wrote *The Thomas Berryman Number.*

I did the first draft in pencil.

But then I typed. The two-finger minuet. I had to reach up to the counter to peck at the keys of my faithful Underwood Champion. Eventually, I hurt my back. That's when I stopped typing and started writing everything in pencil again.

I still write in pencil. I'm writing this with a number 2 pencil. The pencils were gifts from my old friend Tom McGoey. They each say *Alex Cross Lives Here.* My handwriting is impossible to read—even for me. Hell, *I'm* not sure what I just wrote.

After about a thousand revisions, when I thought the manuscript for *The Thomas Berryman Number* might be ready for human consumption, I mailed it out myself. No agent. No early readers. No compelling pitch letter.

I got rejections. Mostly form letters. A couple of handwritten notes from editors that were encouraging. One publisher, Morrow, held on to the manuscript for two months before rejecting it. With a form letter.

Then I read an article in the *New York Times Book Review* about the literary agency Sanford Greenburger Associates. Sanford Greenburger, the founder of the agency, had died in 1971. His son Francis took over the business. Francis was in his twenties, not much older than me. The article in the *Times* said they were accepting manuscripts from unpublished writers. That would be me.

I sent over the manuscript that had already been rejected thirty times. We're talking four hundred typewritten pages secured in a cardboard box. Two days later, I got a phone call from Greenburger Associates. I'm thinking to myself, *I can't believe they turned my book down so fast!*

The caller turned out to be Francis himself. He said, "No, no, no, I'm not turning your novel down. Just the opposite. Come on over and see me. I want to sell this thing. I *will* sell your book."

So Francis hooked me up with Jay Acton, a hot young editor at Thomas Crowell, a small, family-owned New York publisher. Jay and I got along beautifully. He worked with me for about a month on the manuscript. He helped the book take shape and we cut some fat.

Then Jay rejected it. My thirty-first rejection.

But Francis Greenburger talked me down off a ledge of the thirty-story Graybar Building, where J. Walter Thompson had its offices. "Don't worry your pretty little head. I'm going to sell it this week."

And he sold it to Little, Brown. *That week*.

starting at the top

THE EDITOR WHO bought *The Thomas Berryman Number* at Little, Brown was the legendary Ned Bradford, a big deal, a star in the publishing world. Ned Bradford had worked with Norman Mailer, John Fowles, Herman Wouk, and pretty much every major writer that Little, Brown published in those days. And now he was working with twenty-six-year-old me.

Of course, I never felt I was worthy of being included in the same paragraph with Mailer, Fowles, and Herman Wouk. But, hey, all four of us are in *this* paragraph.

In those days, Little, Brown was located on Beacon Street in Boston. It was winter when I visited their offices in this picturesque brick town house called the Cabot Mansion. A very proper but also sweet receptionist brought me to the library room.

There was a fire blazing. She gave me some tea. It was perfect. I'm not kidding you—*perfect.*

I walked around the library, light-headed, proud as could be, stunned that I was there. Not completely believing I was.

On the library shelves were *The French Lieutenant's Woman, The Catcher in the Rye,* several Norman Mailer books. I'm thinking to myself, *Holy shit. This is the best moment of my life. No matter what happens after today, they can't take this away from me.*

It definitely was the best moment of my life—just being allowed in that library room, waiting for my famous editor, Ned Bradford, to come down, see me, and talk for hours about my novel to be published at *the* Little, Brown, one of America's most prestigious publishing houses.

Bradford came down the stairs. On time. We put on our overcoats and he took me around the corner to a famous Boston restaurant, the Locke-Ober Café. In the main dining room hung *Mlle. Yvonne,* a Tommaso Juglaris nude. Even in the 1970s, women could not sit at the bar, although they could eat in the restaurant. I thought it was a crazy rule, but I wasn't going to make a scene about it.

Ned Bradford told me he'd sent *The Thomas Berryman Number*—my novel about a black politician in the South targeted by a professional assassin—out for author quotes. Then he showed me the first response he'd gotten.

I set down the fork I was using to eat my perfectly prepared Dover fricking sole at Locke-Ober. I began to read, then quickly reread.

The author who'd sent the blurb was John D. MacDonald, who wrote the Travis McGee mystery series. MacDonald was famous and very well respected. What he wrote about my novel sent a shiver right through me. John D. MacDonald said, "I'm quite sure that James Patterson wrote a million words before he even started this novel."

I was twenty-six years old, so the million-words part wasn't exactly true, but what a compliment to receive. Maybe I was going to be a writer after all.

Maybe.

But not yet.

norman mailer and
james baldwin—fisticuffs

MY FIRST NEW YORK literary party taught me that, like a lot of secret societies, the inner world of literary people was borderline crazy and completely overrated.

That first lit party was at the home of Jay Acton, the editor who had helped me with but then rejected *The Thomas Berryman Number*. Jay and I had stayed friends and I liked him tremendously.

(Years later, the weirdest thing happened to Jay. He'd switched over to being a literary agent, and one of his clients was bestselling romance writer Helen Van Slyke. She was a friend and also a big moneymaker for Jay. Then Jay got the terrible news that Helen had died, suddenly and apparently without much warning. Next, Jay got some very different news. Helen Van Slyke had left Jay pretty much everything. Suddenly he was rich. I think he bought a minor-league baseball team and a radio station.)

I remember sitting in Jay's living room the night of that party. It was before *Berryman* was actually published. I was in the middle of a conversation with Wilfrid Sheed, whose novel *People Will Always Be Kind* I'd read and loved.

Sheed was, well, *kind*.

He gave me the best advice as I waited for *The Thomas Berryman Number* to be published. "Write another book. Start tonight. You can—" We were interrupted midsentence by some kind of hubbub happening elsewhere in the apartment. People were filing back into a rear hallway. I excused myself and followed the noise and the crowd.

I entered a large bedroom.

The room was packed with people. Noisy people. Sweating people. Tense people. *Fight fans!*

In the middle of the room stood these two small men. They were arguing loudly, fists clenched, looking like they were ready to rumble. The bedroom had become a pint-size boxing ring.

The men were Norman Mailer and James

Baldwin. Two little guys who looked about as athletic as French poodles. Especially Baldwin. I remembered that Mailer had actually done some prizefighting, but he didn't look like much of a fighter to me. The two men were squared off at center ring.

Mailer and Baldwin were arguing about what should be considered good literature and what shouldn't. It seemed clear they weren't big fans of one another. Weird, because I was a fan of both of them, especially James Baldwin.

You could not have dragged me out of that noisy, stuffy, overcrowded bedroom. No fisticuffs yet, but lots of heated words. The literary crowd gathered in the room was *abuzz*. The pugilists were circling, looking for an opportunity to pounce, maybe throw the first punch, but definitely win the war of words.

I have to admit, I found the whole thing hilarious. But I knew I would never forget that scene, and obviously, I haven't.

It set the tone for the absurdity of literary warfare—which I've tried my best to avoid.

Wilfrid Sheed may have written *People Will Always Be Kind*, but I learned that wasn't always the case.

in the days when people actually used landlines

MY STORY AS a writer changed with a single phone call in the spring of 1977.

A woman representing the Mystery Writers of America was on the line. I was busy writing ads at J. Walter. She told me she was calling about the Edgar Allan Poe Awards, known as the Edgars, which were to be presented at a ceremony in New York that weekend.

She sounded a little out of sorts, almost like she was mad at me. "We haven't been able to find you," she said with a huff and a sigh.

I wasn't exactly lost, so I didn't know why she couldn't find me, but now she had me. And then she had my undivided attention. "James, you're a finalist in the Best First Mystery Novel category at the Edgars. I mean, your novel *The Thomas Berryman Number* is a finalist."

I got that part. But honestly, I wondered if

the call was maybe a practical joke. I started thinking about which one of my friends could be the joker. Meanwhile, the woman on the phone was giving me the date and time of the award ceremony.

I knew immediately that I had a work conflict. I told her I couldn't go. I apologized.

"No, no, no, *you're a finalist,*" she repeated a couple of times. "For an Edgar." I told her again that I couldn't go. Burt Manning wouldn't allow it. I actually needed the paycheck from my job in hell.

"You have to go," she finally said. "You won!"

"I *what?*"

So I went to the Edgars—with my parents, Charles and Isabelle. Charles seemed proud, which was nice. He and Isabelle got dressed to the nines and they were beaming all night. Sitting in the audience, even with the heads-up that I'd won, I kept thinking, *Maybe the woman on the phone lied to get me here.*

But I did win. I remember it all as clearly as if it happened yesterday.

Let me give you some perspective about my very short and to-the-point acceptance speech that night at the Edgars. It was my experience at the time that if somebody asked you what you did, and you said you were a writer, the next questions would inevitably be something like "What have you published? Have I read any of your work? Do you publish under your own name or under a pseudonym?" If you then said you were *unpublished,* the person would look at you like you were a fraud and a liar.

So when I went up on the stage to accept my Edgar, all I could think to say was, and this is a direct quote, "I guess I'm a writer now."

robert parker's spenser

THAT'S THE WAY I felt, and those are the words that just came out of my mouth. And it's all I said at the podium that night. *I guess I'm a writer now.*

The audience clapped. My dad actually whistled. Yay for my mom and dad. Yay for me.

After the awards ceremony came some photo ops. I was a little weak in the knees as I stood beside Robert B. Parker, who had won the Best Novel award for *Promised Land*. I'd read every novel in his mystery series, including *Promised Land*.

So I was nervous, and I was shy, and I completely blanked on the name of his main character. I told him so.

Robert Parker snapped back, "Spenser. Like the poet."

I recognized the line immediately. He'd used it in every single Spenser novel.

Afterward, I went out to dinner with my parents—only to find Robert Parker and his family sitting across the room at the same restaurant. I finally walked over to his table. "Spenser, like the poet," I said. Parker laughed and shook my hand.

I continued to read the Spenser novels until Robert Parker died. For me, Spenser died then too. I hope the same will be said of Alex Cross—preferably around 2050.

That weekend of the Edgar Awards, my father wanted to go to P. J. Clarke's, a well-known pub on Third Avenue. We went together. Just Dad and me.

Two tables away sat the playwright Tennessee Williams. My father freaked. He wasn't the type who lost his cool often, but he'd also always wanted to be a writer, and now he was sitting ten feet or less from one of his idols. *A Streetcar Named Desire* and *Cat on a Hot Tin Roof* were Charles's favorite plays.

Even though my father desperately wanted to talk to the playwright, he didn't. He wouldn't think of bothering the great Tennessee Williams.

It was an unforgettable moment, one of my best with my father. We had bonded over a writer we both admired. And Dad had been at my side when I became a writer.

new york writers walk the walk

NEW YORK IS a walking town—at least, it was until the virus came and tried to kill all eight million of us.

Instead of taking lunch while I was at Thompson, I used to go on long walks. I must have passed Woody Allen on the street a dozen times. I'd give a little half wave. He'd occasionally half-wave back. We never spoke. Ah, the writers' brother- and sisterhood.

Another writer I saw on my daily walks was Kurt Vonnegut. I was surprised that Vonnegut was such a big guy. I don't like to bother people, but one of the times I saw him, I finally introduced myself. He didn't know my work, but I knew his. Vonnegut and I sat on the steps of an East Side brownstone and shot the breeze one sunny afternoon in the early winter. I'd read just about all of his books. So we talked about *God Bless You, Mr. Rosewater* and *Cat's Cradle,* then photography and movies.

I remember that we talked about a mutual favorite, Richard Brautigan, who wrote *Trout Fishing in America,* which was not about fishing. Vonnegut was funny and seemed kooky, but there was a sadness about him, a little like his literary alter ego Kilgore Trout. The success of *Slaughterhouse Five,* the first of his novels to feature Trout, apparently drove him to attempt suicide. *So it goes.*

I will always remember something Vonnegut wrote in *God Bless You, Mr. Rosewater.* "Hello, babies. Welcome to Earth. It's hot in the summer and cold in the winter. It's round and wet and crowded. At the outside, babies, you've got about a hundred years here. There's only one rule that I know of, babies—'God damn it, you've got to be kind.'"

Vonnegut told me he hadn't read *People Will Always Be Kind,* so I sent him a copy through his publisher. But I never saw him again after that day on the brownstone steps.

By the way, after we talked, he walked inside the brownstone. He lived there. Or maybe he was breaking in. Who could tell with Kurt Vonnegut? Or was it Kilgore Trout I'd been talking to?

america tells the truth, finally

MY FIRST ROOTIN'-TOOTIN', honest-to-God *New York Times* bestseller was actually a nonfiction book called *The Day America Told the Truth.* On some level, that seemed like a joke. Little, Brown had passed on it, so Richard Pine, my intrepid agent at that time, took it around to other publishers and sold it to McGraw Hill. In 1991, the book hit the *Times* bestseller list. That drove Little, Brown more than a little crazy, especially my fiction editor and friend Fredi Friedman—who was very smart, and also very competitive.

My partner on that nonfiction book was Peter Kim, the head of research at J. Walter Thompson. Peter and I were best buddies. When the book came out, we appeared on *The Oprah Winfrey Show,* which was a very big deal in the publishing world.

Peter Kim was a brilliant guy whose family had escaped from North Korea in the sixties. They wound up living in Iowa, of all places, which Peter actually loved. He went on to graduate from NYU—at nineteen.

The very sad thing about my friend Peter was that he was dying of a heart ailment. Peter knew it. There was nothing he could do. He'd already seen half the specialists in New York. But Peter, being Peter, wanted to keep working. And he continued to be a special friend.

Peter could talk about anything, *anything*. But minutes before the *Oprah* taping, he started mumbling, "Oh my God, Jim, I can't do this. What are we doing here? In Chicago? I think I'm going to throw up. These are *Oprah's people*."

Early in the show Oprah tried her best to ask Peter questions. She threw him softball after softball. He came back with "Yes" or "No." That's a disaster on television. Oprah couldn't believe it and neither could I. The whole thing was captured on national television. I covered as well as I could for my tongue-tied partner.

One day a week, Oprah did two shows. She filmed them at the Chicago Shakespeare Theater on Navy Pier, which is a playhouse in the round. Peter and I were surrounded by a large audience. In our book, we had interviewed people all around America. We'd asked somewhat probing, mostly ridiculous questions, like "For two million dollars, could you give up your faith?"

Oprah threw out the question to her live audience. A woman rose up and said, "I couldn't do it. My faith is too important to me. Not even for two million dollars." Oprah signaled for the audience to applaud and she praised the woman for the strength of her beliefs.

A little later in the show, one of Oprah's questions was "Could you kill a stranger for two million dollars?"

That same woman stood up. She said, "For two million dollars, yes, I could. From a great distance. With a rifle."

Oprah snuck a look at Peter and me. She rolled her eyes and tried her damnedest to hold back a smile. We could all see why this woman needed her church.

Later that same week, Peter and I did Larry King's radio show. Peter had no trouble talking to King. But when the commercials came on, Larry laid his head down on his desk. And he fell asleep.

Peter and I started whispering. "Holy shit, this guy is out cold. What do we do after the commercials? Should I ask you questions, or should you ask me?"

The commercials stopped, and it was probably the first time in my life I didn't want the ads to end.

Then Larry King popped up like a little jack-in-the-box.

"Okay," he said, "I'm here live with James Patterson and Peter Kim. Tell me about the woman in your new book who swore she could kill a stranger for two million dollars."

the jane stories

I LIVED WITH Jane Hall Blanchard for seven years, until she died at thirty-nine. Up until the time I fell for Sue Solie and married her, Jane was the love of my life.

The truth is, Jane totally saved me. She turned me around, turned my life around, changed my view of myself. I was basically this insecure knucklehead from upstate, and I didn't really know how to behave in polite society, at least not in New York City society, not even while I was rising fast at J. Walter Thompson and writing novels on the side. Jane's family had some money and some manners and, most important, confidence. And Jane was always so considerate, so human, never impatient with me.

Early on in our relationship, she asked me to go to a four-star French restaurant with her. Once we were seated, she could tell I was uncomfortable. It wasn't hard to figure out. My body was as stiff as a mannequin in Macy's window. I was extremely quiet and had trouble forcing a smile. I didn't know much about French menus and I honestly didn't know how to act in this very formal, upscale Manhattan eating place.

It was Jane's favorite restaurant in New York, and she wanted to share it with me, but she was cool about my uneasiness. She had ordered some kind of French stew, her favorite dish there. Suddenly, she plopped her face down into the stew and came up with brown goop all over her nose, cheeks, and mouth. Then Jane said to me, "You need to know something, Jimmy. This is *our* place. This is *our* restaurant. We belong here."

She didn't say it loudly, and she didn't lower her face into the plate in a way that would offend anyone around us. Her movie-worthy gesture was just for me.

This is our place. We belong. You belong. So chill out.

And Jane did it in such a kind way, with her usual humor. There was no implied criticism. That's the kind of person she was.

A while later, I did a year in therapy. It was valuable as hell. I saw a terrific doctor, a great, smart guy to talk to, once a week. Ultimately, he became a friend. After I stopped seeing him as a doctor, we'd go out to lunch once or twice a month. He even paid half the time. Maybe 40 percent of the time.

He got me more in touch with myself. I had some anger issues and he helped me see that the anger mostly had to do with my father. He helped me understand that the way I was acting wasn't really me, it was my father. I also realized I didn't have to blame my father. My poor dad had his own tough issues and probably felt he was doing the best he could. The year of therapy helped me understand that I was, well, lovable—not because I was first in my class, not because I was successful as hell, but because I was me. Basically, a reasonably nice person who mostly tries to do the right thing.

And that was another thing about Jane. She loved *me*. I couldn't help wondering, *Why?* But she did.

Early on in our relationship, we took it slow. Jane and I would get together after work. We'd go to a movie, go to a restaurant, or just do nothing. She did some home cooking. But every time she'd see me, she would totally light up. She'd wave both arms over her head. She'd call out my name. Even on a crowded New York street. She could be silly and get me to be silly and give her a big smile. I'm not one of the world's best smilers, but Jane could get me smiling every time. That smile lasted for seven years.

still jane

WHEN JANE AND I started going out, she was a pack-a-day smoker. My parents both smoked, so I was accustomed to it, but I didn't like it. I could never get used to that awful, acrid smell. One morning before we went to work, Jane announced, "I'm not going to smoke anymore. I'm done with that filthy habit. I'm finished." She was going to do it cold turkey too.

To celebrate, I cooked dinner that night. To put it mildly, I'm not the greatest cook, but I prepared what was, for me, a gourmet meal. I got out Jane's good silver, lit half a dozen candles, the whole romantic shebang. It was a big dinner for us: roast chicken, haricots verts, mashed potatoes, gravy, even a chocolate cake *made from scratch*—my grandmother's recipe.

We sat down at the table, and Jane's smile lit up the room. This was perfect!

She took one bite of the chicken and burst into tears. I turned white and started apologizing. How had I screwed up roast chicken so badly? Jane dashed across the living room and grabbed her purse. She lit up a cigarette. "I thought I could. I thought I was ready. I'm so sorry, Jimmy."

Two weeks later, she did quit, and she stayed with it. Jane never smoked again.

One Saturday morning not long after that, Jane and I went out to breakfast near where we lived on the West Side of New York. After coffee, bagels, and eggs, we stopped at the post office on Columbus, the Ansonia Station.

Once we were inside, Jane fell to the floor and started shaking terribly. She was in great pain. We both thought she was dying. A nurse happened to be in the post office. She rushed over to help Jane. "I think your"—I don't know if she said *wife* or *friend*—"is having a seizure."

Jane finally stopped shaking and she managed to sit up on the floor, but we were both terrified. And totally mystified. We started consulting doctors around New York. We found out that Jane had a brain tumor.

She had surgery at New York Hospital, one

of the best places in the world for cancer treatment. They removed most of the tumor, but they couldn't get it all. We were told that Jane was going to die, probably within the next year. She was thirty-six.

She never complained, never shook her fist at the heavens, never once asked, *Why me?* She spent weeks and sometimes months in the hospital during the two and a half years that she lived. She had lots and lots of visitors and she never wanted to bring her friends and family down, not even while she was getting chemo and her hair was falling out. She had a collection of funny, goofy-looking hats that she'd wear. A different hat almost every day. The hat-of-the-day never failed to get her visitors laughing and then Jane would laugh too. That's just who she was.

I had never been more in love with anybody. I was wildly in love with this woman who had to use a walker or wheelchair and had clumps of hair sprouting all over her head. It taught me something about the importance we tend to put on physical appearance. Imagine going on a blind date, and the person who shows up is using a walker and losing her hair. Not too many of us would have a second date. But during those days, I was more in love with Jane than I'd ever been. She was my best friend, the love of my life up to that point, and she was a saint.

During that time, I was running the Burger King business, which was the biggest account at J. Walter Thompson. After Jane got sick with that hellacious disease, I refused to travel. I wouldn't go on film shoots. I wouldn't go to Miami for meetings at Burger King headquarters. I convinced them that the business ran best with me staying in the ad factory, making sure that the work was as good as it could possibly be. The Burger King folk—especially Kyle Craig and Jeff Campbell—were good clients, good people. Besides that, they all loved Jane too.

still jane, for another couple of minutes

I WASN'T REALLY surprised that Jane beat the expectations of her doctors. No matter the setbacks—including three long stays at New York Hospital—she was always upbeat. Her spirit was amazing. I don't know how she did it, but she was a role model for everybody who knew her. Several of our friends in those days named their babies "Jane" in her honor.

Jane's parents had a place on the Jersey Shore. That's where Jane spent her last summer. She was in a wheelchair most of the time, but she loved being at the ocean. I would come to the shore every weekend and try to make it a three-day weekend if I could.

One Sunday, I was going up the beach road in a taxi, pointed toward the train station in Mantoloking, heading to New York. I couldn't help looking back through the cab's rear window. I didn't want to take my eyes off Jane.

She was out on the street in her wheelchair, smiling, waving to me, getting smaller and smaller and smaller.

I never forgot that image. Not even now. I'm still watching her get smaller. Every time I had to leave Jane, I wondered if I would ever see her again.

Her neurologist at New York Hospital, Frank Petito, was a great guy and he loved Jane. He would arrive at his office early in the morning, see patients, then routinely work until ten o'clock at night. At one point during Jane's illness, I developed Bell's palsy and Frank saw me as a patient.

After he finished for the night, he usually came to Jane's room. He'd put his feet up on her bed, sit with us, and we'd talk about anything and everything and nothing at all for ten or fifteen minutes. Talking with Jane and me was his way to unwind. Also, she usually kept Godiva chocolates hidden away for Petito. She knew his favorites. Jane knew everybody's favorites.

During this period, every day was on the scary side of tense and dramatic. My blood pressure had always been normal, but suddenly it shot up 30 to 40 points. I got that scary Bell's palsy for a couple of weeks.

Then, one morning when I was at work, I got a call from the hospital. Jane's younger sister, sweet, sweet Sarah, was on the line. She told me that Jane was having a bad time that morning. This was probably it. I rushed uptown to New York Hospital. Sarah and Jane's mother, Anne, was also in her room. So was Dr. Frank Petito. They all seemed so small, ethereal, almost otherworldly.

I'm so glad I got there when I did. I was holding Jane's hand when she passed. When she heard me whispering up against her cheek, she squeezed my hand twice. Then she was gone. I can barely write these words, even now, after all this time.

writer's block

I FOUND IT impossible to write after Jane died. Her death, her not being there anymore—not seeing her face, not hearing her voice—had a numbing effect on me. I was out of it all the time. A deep sadness fell over me, a depressing fog that stayed with me day and night, weekdays and through the very long weekends. When I finally tried to write again, the pages were so awful, I didn't even try to get them published.

When my grandfather had died back in Newburgh, I'd felt something like this. I remember going to my grandparents' house after he died, walking in the deep woods where I used to tell stories to myself as a spacey little kid, unable to cry about Pop's death. *I could not cry. For years and years, I could not cry. Could not, even when I desperately wanted to.*

But after Jane died, I cried every day. This went on for a year, maybe more than a year. Sometimes I'd force the tears to come. Late at night in our apartment on Central Park West, I would put on a favorite song of ours. I thought of it as the pleasure of grieving. I'm not sure *pleasure* is the correct word. Maybe it's *relief,* the relief of grieving, of being able to feel something, even intense sadness.

Whatever it is, I have never been able to really say goodbye to her.

Goodbye, Janie.

It still doesn't work.

alexis cross

I FINALLY STARTED a love story, a saga with mystery elements. Halfway through my initial draft, I experienced my first and only bout of writer's block. I couldn't get my head or, especially, my heart into the novel. Even after it was finished—and I mean *finished*—I never submitted it to publishers. Eventually, I destroyed the pages. And *no,* I don't regret it. And *yes,* I really did shred the original. I don't remember anything about the story, not a scene, not one character, not even the book's title.

As I've said, I finally threw myself into the Mad Men world and rose from copywriter to creative director to CEO. I was done as a novelist. I wasn't a writer anymore. It was the late 1980s and three years since my previous novel had been published.

But honestly, I couldn't help myself. I finally

took up my pencil and wrote a mystery novel called *The Midnight Club*, which was how I got back to Little, Brown. It was also how I met the producers David Brown and Joe Wizan. They optioned the book and promised me they would get the movie made.

Next, I started a very pacey thriller about a Washington, DC, homicide detective, Alexis Cross. Sixty pages in, the story wasn't working. More writer's block? That was my fear. Then Alexis became Alex, and suddenly the novel, *Along Came a Spider*, seemed to write itself.

I think I know why. When I started to conceptualize *Along Came a Spider*, I wrote a full-length outline of the story. Several hundred pages. When I went back to start the novel itself, I realized that *I had already written it.* The short chapters in the long outline seemed just right to me, a way of keeping *Along Came a Spider* bright and hot from beginning to end. This reminded me of a story I'd heard from my editor Michael Pietsch about Bruce Springsteen: When Springsteen was writing *Nebraska*, he put down a demo, just him and his acoustic guitar. He eventually realized that the demo *was* the record. In the same vein, I came to understand that my long outline for

Along Came a Spider essentially *was* the novel. It was also the birth of a new writing style for me. I had discovered that the pace, the drama, should never stop.

When I submitted *Along Came a Spider,* Larry Kirshbaum was the head of Time Warner Books, which included Little, Brown. Larry had a really good feel for commercial fiction. He and his team discovered David Baldacci, Nicholas Sparks, and me.

Larry read *Along Came a Spider* on a plane headed to London. As soon as he finished, he handed the manuscript over to his number two, who was sitting beside him. When they arrived in England, Larry called Fredi Friedman—my editor at the time—and they made a seven-figure offer for two Alex Cross novels, *Along Came a Spider* and *Kiss the Girls.*

I didn't know it yet, but I was about to get star treatment at Little, Brown. When a publisher offers a writer seven figures, the execs go all out to make the book work.

And it worked beautifully for *Along Came a Spider.* The reviews were very good, especially one George Pelecanos wrote in the *Washington Post. Along Came a Spider* made it to number 2 on the *New York Times* bestseller list.

I didn't feel particularly deserving of this sudden fame and fortune, but I was sure liking it. There's nothing like walking by a bookstore and seeing a couple of your novels staring back at you from the front window.

speaking of bookstore windows

OKAY, I AM walking along Broadway in New York City. I'm walking pretty quickly. I arrive at my local Barnes & Noble on the corner of Sixty-Seventh Street. I see three copies of my novel *Along Came a Spider* in the window. This is good stuff.

I've been pretty much waiting for this to happen since I first came to live in New York in the 1970s. It's now January of 1993.

I go inside the bookstore. I'm hyperventilating a little. I want to make this moment last.

It's a Sunday. I've just seen that *Along Came a Spider* is number 6 on the *New York Times* bestseller list. I don't think that could be a mistake, but I'm a little afraid it might be.

I walk toward the fiction section and I can already see the cover for *Along Came a*

Spider. It features big type and an illustration of a spider hanging over a suburban-looking house.

Now here's what some writers do. We count the number of copies of our book in stock at the local bookstore.

I know there were twelve copies of *Along Came a Spider* here a few days ago. Now there are six copies.

So maybe the *New York Times* bestseller list is accurate. I'm feeling a little dizzy. I don't know how to handle this. I'm starting to get hopeful—and hope is not a strategy.

While I'm heading toward *Along Came a Spider*, a woman picks up a copy.

I stop walking.

Now, here's another thing that happens with some writers: If we see you pick up a copy of one of our books at the store, we watch you. If you buy the book, I swear, it makes our whole day. But if you put the book down, reject us, as it were, it breaks our hearts. Seriously. I think it hurts our souls.

So I'm watching this woman, practicing spy craft the way I've read about it in John le Carré mysteries.

She reads the flap copy, then she reads the

author blurbs on the back cover. Then she puts *Along Came a Spider* under her arm.

I'm trying to be cool about this, but I want to go over and give her a big hug.

I watch this wonderful, wonderful person walk down a long, narrow aisle—and then she slides *Along Came a Spider* into her hobo bag.

She stole the book.

And all I can think is *Does that count as a sale?*

the book-tour boogie

IN THOSE EARLY days, I wrote an Alex Cross book every year. That's it. Just one novel. What a slacker I was.

But I was starting to be kind of a minor big-deal writer and I got to go on book tours. Very large book tours. As many cities as I was game to visit. Sometimes I would do *three* five-hundred-to one-thousand-person signings in a day.

The cool thing was that most of the people who came to the signings really liked my writing. They especially loved Alex Cross and, eventually, Lindsay Boxer and the Women's Murder Club. And then young adults got into the Maximum Ride series.

I visited Lexington, Kentucky, on one of the tours. There was a very long line snaking around the Joseph-Beth bookstore. I sign books quickly, talking all the while, but this was going to be a two- to three-hour event.

At around the halfway point, an attractive,

nicely dressed woman edged up to the signing table. She spoke in a soft voice, almost a whisper. I noticed that her hands were trembling. I leaned in and asked her if she was all right.

She said she was fine; she was great, actually. Just very nervous. Then she confessed that *Along Came a Spider* was the first book that she'd ever read in her life. She hadn't even learned to read until her early twenties. She thanked me and said she was a big reader now. Then she started to cry, and we held hands for a few seconds. I thanked *her* for coming and told her she had made my day. She really had. I've never forgotten our minutes together at Joseph-Beth.

Every day on the tour brought new surprises, both good and bad.

I have signed Nook covers, Kindle covers, bookstore sales slips, backs of hands, breasts, sneakers, menus, golf balls, baseballs, and hundreds of ball caps...yes, I've signed breasts. Golf balls actually present more of a challenge. They're so small, so round, so hard. *Are you reading this, Tiger Woods? Are you nodding your head and smiling a little?*

In Fort Worth, Texas, I reluctantly agreed to autograph a sheet that was going in the coffin of the husband of a very persuasive and bereaved widow.

A sweet fourteen-year-old in Boston asked me to sign and personalize *Suzanne's Diary for Nicholas,* her grandmother's favorite novel. That afternoon the girl was heading to a local funeral home to put the book in her grandma's casket before she was buried.

I went on a TV show one time in Birmingham, Alabama, which is the home of Books-A-Million. The host said that he hadn't read *Suzanne's Diary for Nicholas,* the book I was there to promote, but he'd given it to his wife the night before. He had gone off to bed and left her reading.

As he told me live on Birmingham TV, "My wife came into our bedroom at two this morning. She apologized for waking me. Then she said the most amazing thing: 'I'm sorry for getting you up, but I just finished that book, and I had to come in here and tell you how much I love you!'"

Some coldhearted folks might roll their eyes, but I find that kind of emotion hard to come by and hard to resist. Maybe it's just the small-town kid in me bubbling up again, but that's my deal.

book tours, they just won't go away

AUTHOR TOURS AREN'T as glamorous as you might think, not even if you're John Grisham or James Patterson.

You fly into Boston, or Charlotte, or Miami, or Phoenix, Charleston, San Francisco—but usually all you get to see is some mall with a big chain store. Maybe a charming side street with an independent bookstore.

And the local radio station, of course. Lots of radio stations. And lots of DJs who haven't read your book, so they'll start the interview like this: "James, tell us what the new book is about."

The people who chauffeur you around are known as escorts. (Not that kind of escort. Although my friend Nelson DeMille's second and third marriages were to book-tour escorts. Hey, it gets lonely out there on the road.) Most of them are friendly, talkative, and helpful, and they're almost always book lovers.

The escorts will gladly tell you all about their city. I always ask, "Who's the nicest author you've ever brought around town?" Hands down, it was the late Mary Higgins Clark. "And who is the worst?" Two names came up again and again. One was a fabulously successful Brit novelist, the other a thriller writer from Norway. I'll leave it at that.

I've never had much trouble on the road—in fact, most of the crowds are enthusiastic and fun to hang out with. Hey, they're fans. One time in DC, though, this one guy asked question after question after my talk. I signed a lot of books, then I snuck out the store's back door with the Little, Brown public relations person, Heather Rizzo.

The same guy was hanging out next to our car. *Shit.* Then it got worse.

He wanted to show me his favorite new gun, and that's what he did. I'm not really a gun person, but he was holding a Glock 43X. He gave me the rundown. "Fills up your palm, James. Great carry gun. Good stopping power."

At this point, Heather and I wanted to get the hell out of, well, Dodge.

I kept smiling and talking. "Nice. Great carry gun. Alex Cross uses a Glock. No, no, no. I don't need to hold it. I'm good. We have to run to the airport. See you next time we're in town. Lower your weapon."

Actually, the next time I did a signing in Washington was with President Clinton, and he brought the Secret Service. They brought along their own guns.

While I'm on the subject of book tours, two of my favorite public relations people deserve a shout-out. Heather Rizzo guided me around the country for years. She now works with Michael Connelly. *Smart*. Erinn McGrath is currently my very wise and patient handler, as she was during the somewhat turbulent whirl-wind tour with President Clinton, when Erinn really earned her stars and stripes.

change is good, but change is hard

IN THE SPRING of 1999, I asked for a meeting with the brass at Little, Brown. I was selling a lot of books by then, so I got the meeting. The publisher, Larry Kirshbaum, had become a close friend of mine. He still is. We lunch at Patroon, Stuart Woods's fictional hero Stone Barrington's favorite eating and drinking spot in New York City.

I'd been writing a mystery novel a year, and the Little, Brown execs had it all programmed on their little spreadsheets. Now I told them I wanted them to consider a change—a big change for the entire publishing business, as it turned out.

I took a breath, then told the Little, Brown elites my idea. "I want to write two, maybe three books a year." No audible gasps came from the august group, but I detected skepticism and at least one wrinkled brow.

I gave them three ideas for new books. One was for the Alex Cross series, one was a twisty beach mystery called *The Beach House,* and one was a love story, *Suzanne's Diary for Nicholas.*

During the meeting, I told them how the story for *Suzanne's Diary* came to be. At that time, my wife, Sue, had already taken about five hundred thousand photographs, maybe a million, of our baby son, Jack. A couple of thick photo albums were sitting on a table in our living room.

One afternoon I started leafing through them. It struck me that at some point, Jack might be looking at the same photo album, but Sue and I would be gone. Then I had a much worse thought. I imagined Sue and I going through the same album—if Jack somehow died before us. That's how *Suzanne's Diary for Nicholas* came to be.

I told the Little, Brown executives the story, and Larry Kirshbaum teared up. His instincts were usually very good. He immediately got the power of *Suzanne's Diary for Nicholas.*

Then Larry gave me his thoughts and his decision on the three books. "We love the Alex Cross, of course. And *The Beach House* sounds fabulous. But *Suzanne's Diary*, Jim, that just isn't your brand."

That struck me as an interesting comment. I was the one with the big rep for watching over *brands* like Ford, Burger King, Kodak, and Warner-Lambert. I was pretty sure I understood brands as well as anybody in the room. Or in the building, for that matter. So I wrote *Suzanne's Diary* anyway. Little, Brown published it. It became one of my top-selling books ever.

If you haven't read it, now's as good a time as any.

Go on, get out of here. Head out to a bookstore. Or go online.

Yeah, *you*.

In the words of Truman Capote, "A boy has to sell his books."

ohhhhk-lahoma!

REMEMBER THE BROADWAY musical and movie *Oklahoma!*? This story has almost nothing to do with either except that it takes place in Oklahoma.

When I started to hit the bestseller lists, Little, Brown assigned me a very sharp PR person named Holly Wilkinson. Her grandfather was Bud Wilkinson, the legendary Oklahoma University football coach. Bud Wilkinson won three national championships. He was the Nick Saban of his day. Holly told me that. Several times, actually.

She was always trying to trick me into visiting bookstores in Oklahoma. Finally, she just wore me down.

So I headed out to Oklahoma with Holly. As it happened, an old buddy of mine from St. Patrick's High School lived somewhere in the Sooner State. Danny Boudreau had been a wild man when I knew him as a kid in Newburgh. I figured he was probably working on oil rigs, but I was pretty sure he'd be doing something completely off the charts. As it turned out, he was.

My first night in Oklahoma, I got back to the hotel late after a book signing. I called the phone number I had gotten for wildcatter Danny.

I got a recording.

The woman on the line sounded very official and impressive. I was stunned by what she had to say. I was flabbergasted. "This is the office of Daniel Boudreau, justice of the Oklahoma Supreme Court." And I'm thinking, *This is crazy. Poor Oklahoma. Poor Sooners. Way to fool 'em, Danny.*

The next day, the two of us met for lunch. Danny wasn't Danny anymore. He no longer looked away when he talked to you. Nor did he lay his head down sideways on the table while he ate (which he'd done at my parents' house one night when we were little kids). He was confident; he was well spoken; he was humorous; he was a great guy. Still, I kind of missed Newburgh Danny.

fire in the hole

ON YET ANOTHER book tour, I was supposed to fly from LA to San Francisco at around nine one night. Unfortunately, San Francisco was completely fogged in. I finally got to my hotel in San Fran at two in the morning.

I was picked up by an escort at six a.m. We did three morning-radio interviews and one cable TV appearance.

Finally, around eleven, I told the escort that I had to go back to the St. Regis and get some sleep. I still had two signings, big ones, in front of me that day.

Back at the hotel, groggy, a little grumpy, I checked my voice messages. At that time, I had a beach house on the Jersey Shore. A local Realtor had left a message. It was brief and concise and devastating.

"Mr. Patterson, your beach house is on fire!"

In that instant, I went from unable to keep my eyes open to *wide awake!*

As it turned out, the situation at my shore house couldn't possibly have been worse. Tony Peyser was the one who visited what was left, because I didn't really want to see the heart-breaking ruins myself. Only *half* of the house had burned down. Terrible for me, good for the insurance company. They looked at it as a big positive that half my house was still standing. They suggested that we play Let's Make a Deal. So I sold my beloved house. Half of it, anyway. And I got half of a good price.

sorry, i'm not jay-z

I SPEAK AT colleges as often as I can. It's great. Invigorating. Challenging. You know how it goes, though. Every single kid in college is smarter than you are. Their favorite line seems to be "You don't understand."

Once when I visited a New York City school, a student representing the English department met me in the parking lot. He looked thoroughly puzzled.

Finally, he squeezed out the question that was obviously buzzing around in his brain. "Um, uh, Mr. Patterson, *where's your entourage?*"

I shrugged. "Hey, it's just me. I'm here alone. I even parked my own car. Been doing it for years. Let's go talk about books."

The kid just stood there and he kept shaking his head. He couldn't believe I'd come there by myself. "You are James Patterson, right?" he finally asked.

I borrowed Jess Corman's funny line from my J. Walter Thompson days. "Why? Does he owe you money?"

The kid didn't get it.

That reminds me of something. At different speaking events, I've heard the same line at least a dozen times: "You look taller on your book-jacket photos." *Huh?* I'm around five eleven; at least, I used to be. On the book jackets, I think I'm about, I don't know, nine inches tall. Seven inches on the paperbacks.

One time at an airport bookstore, I stood in line to buy a couple of books and some bubble gum. I was behind a woman and I noticed she had one of my novels in her basket. I said something like "Oh, you're going to read one of my books."

The woman would not believe that I was me. I finally had to pull out my wallet. I showed her my photo ID.

She still didn't believe me.

She put my book back too.

That hurt.

people actually read in sweden

SWEDEN HAS A population of a little over eight million people, and its most successful books sell half a million copies. People read in Sweden. They particularly love mystery novels. That's true all over Scandinavia.

I cowrote a mystery with a smart, engaging, enormously popular Swedish author, Liza Marklund. *The Postcard Killers* told the creepy tale of an eerie murder spree across Europe. The killers were brother and sister and the tone was a little like *The Talented Mr. Ripley*. At least, Liza and I thought so. We're both Patricia Highsmith fans.

When you publish a book in the U.S. nowadays, you're lucky if you get one or two interviews. I'm not kidding. If you are interviewed, the same questions get asked over and over again. You start wondering if the press is just one person. A press clone? There might be a creepy horror novel in that.

It's different in Europe. When I went to Stockholm the week Liza and I published our book, we had forty-seven interviews with newspapers and magazines.

The European interview style is more stimulating and challenging than what I'm used to in America. Reporters ask questions on sociology, history, philosophy, current events that relate to your book. They don't condescend because you've written a "penny dreadful."

There *was* one question that almost all the interviewers asked: "How did a Swede and an American ever get together and agree on things? How is that even possible?"

In interview after interview, Liza and I told them that it was really pretty simple for us. Here was our secret: One, you need to have mutual respect, and Liza and I did. Two, you have to listen to one another. Liza and I listened to each other. I think that's the secret to success in almost everything—*listening*.

Eventually, a movie was made from the novel. In my opinion, the producers of *The Postcard Killings* (they changed the title slightly from the book's) didn't listen. Not to me, anyway. I'm not sure they had much respect either. The film was, to be kind, not very good. The production company asked me to help promote the film. I apologized but told them I couldn't bring myself to do it.

What could I have said? "Watching *The Postcard Killings* gave me the shivers!" But not the good kind.

the murder of stephen king

I THINK THE most useful—maybe even the most important—thing I ever did in publishing wasn't as big a success as it might've been. I wrote or created the outlines for seventy-three BookShots. BookShots were novellas that sold for $4.99. My idea, my theory, my observation, was that a lot of people didn't have the time to read four- and five-hundred-page novels or nonfiction books. But I wanted to keep them reading.

So I created the BookShot, and my publishers—Little, Brown in the United States and Penguin Random House in the UK—bought into the idea. Each BookShot was around a hundred fifty pages and could be read in a couple of hours. Lots of suspense coming at the reader in a hurry, like watching a fast-paced movie.

One of the BookShot novellas was called *The Murder of Stephen King*. It was a nice, twisty story. Believe it or not, Stephen King was the hero, the star. And—spoiler alert—*he doesn't get murdered.*

Okay, okay, *The Murder of Stephen King* was a little wink from me to Uncle Stevie. I figured he could take a little good-natured ribbing. We're both small-town guys, right? No big egos?

As a courtesy, the publisher at Little, Brown let King's people know the book was coming out. The King camp didn't like that. *You can't do this. James shouldn't do this. This would be a terrible thing to do.* Then Stephen King's representative hauled out the heavy artillery. *Does James know that Tabitha King was actually threatened once inside their house by an intruder?*

I didn't know that, and I got the point. But shouldn't that mean that maybe Stephen King should stop writing his own scary stories—if they were genuinely putting his family members in danger. I'm just saying...

Anyway, out of respect, I decided not to publish *The Murder of Stephen King*—a cool story with Stephen King as the damn hero. Little, Brown ate the entire print run. And nobody ever sent a note to say thanks.

I still enjoy King's scary novels. The man can tell a story. But I guess he has trouble with thank-you notes. I'm reading King's *If It Bleeds* now, and I'm a little sorry to report that I'm liking it a lot.

fear of public speaking

IT IS STILL a little painful for me to remember standing in front of an auditorium packed with J. Walter Thompson people, staring down at my notes, and *reading* them line by line. The audience had no idea that I was petrified to be up there.

I finally learned how to overcome my deep fear of public speaking, and I learned it the hard way. I was one of five writers who spoke at a *New York Times*–sponsored event. I *read* from my latest novel, and I bombed. Big time. It was as painful as multiple wasp stings, but I learned something that changed everything about how I talk in front of a group.

Most people, especially adults, don't want to be lectured to, and they definitely don't want to listen to somebody staring down at pages and reading from his or her book. They want to hear stories. And, man, do I have stories to tell.

So I began telling stories whenever I had to speak in front of a crowd. My confidence rose. That's critically important. I once asked Morgan Freeman what the key was to his acting success. "Confidence. That's it. I know the material, and I know I'm going to deliver it well." And he does. *Very well.*

A different kind of public speaking is called for when you act as a moderator. The late-night talk-show host Johnny Carson was about the best I ever saw. He let his guests talk, except when they got stuck. If that happened, Johnny stepped in and basically interviewed himself.

When President Clinton and I toured for *The President Is Missing,* we had a different moderator in every city. Lee Child, Paul Begala, and our lawyer Bob Barnett were great because they were smart enough to ask good questions and then get out of the way. The audience was there to listen to Clinton and, to a lesser extent, me.

On that same book tour, President Clinton told me that he'd read somewhere (he reads *everything*) that the attention span of humans is eight seconds. The attention span of butterflies is nine seconds. I don't know who studies this stuff, but more power to them. I mean, who has the patience to interview butterflies?

Recently, I spoke at a big mystery writers' conference—actually, two of them, one in Harrogate, England, the other in Dallas. I did two talks in Dallas.

The first moderator's questions were so long and self-referential that he took up half our stage time and cut short the Q&A. The second was moderated by crackerjack mystery writer Hank Phillippi Ryan. She was just about perfect. The two of us went back and forth with humor and charm, exactly as it should be.

Interestingly, I hadn't ever played the role of moderator until recently in south Florida. I asked questions of author Leslie Gray Streeter, and I knew my job. That was Leslie's show, not mine. It was about *Black Widow,* her autobiography.

On the other hand, *this* is *my* show.

i want to be bono, if only i could sing on key and was better-looking

ONE NIGHT DURING my salad days in New York, I had seats for a Knicks game in the upper deck at Madison Square Garden. My friend David Hale and I had gone on a beer run and we were returning to our row in the nosebleed section just as the announcer blared over the PA, "And now, our national anthem!"

As it happened, David and I were passing under the American flag. So we stopped there, put our hands over our hearts, and listened to the anthem.

Suddenly, 20,000 people were staring up *at us*—well, this is what it felt like to me—and they were singing their hearts out. It was as if they fricking *loved* us.

Man, I felt what it was like to be Bono from U2, or maybe Springsteen. And I liked it a lot.

But before I go on here, the really big-deal sportswriter Mike Lupica told me his favorite national-anthem story from his days reporting at

Madison Square Garden. The PA announcer at the Garden, John F. X. Condon, bellowed, "And now, Gladys Gooding will play our national anthem." Some wise guy in the crowd shouted, "Gladys Gooding sucks!" John F. X. Condon didn't miss a beat. "Nevertheless, she will now play our national anthem."

Anyway, I've gradually become comfortable speaking in front of very large crowds. President Clinton and I did a couple of events with over 10,000 people. I spoke before 50,000 or more Gators at a University of Florida graduation. It's kind of cool being a rock star. I could get used to it. If only I could sing.

But here was my very best thrill in front of a crowd. It happened at the Children's Choice Book Awards. I had been nominated for the Children's Author of the Year Award. My son, Jack, was around twelve. He'd told me, "No offense, Dad, but Rick Riordan"—author of the Percy Jackson series—"is going to win."

Sue and I took Jack to the awards show anyway. And I won! Jack jumped into my arms and gave me a hug and a kiss. "You did it, Dad! You did it!"

I did indeed. I was Bono for an audience of one, my son, Jack.

outline, outline, outline

ANYTIME I SPEAK to a group, any group, I get asked about my writing process. Sometimes when I'm out with my wife, Sue—at a restaurant, taking a walk around town, at the movies—I get stopped...and asked about my writing process. So maybe you're wondering, *What's James Patterson's writing process?*

I write a fifty- to eighty-page outline. For every book.

I write three or four drafts of every outline.

I write with a pencil. I like being able to erase things and I'm pretty good at admitting when I make a mistake.

At this point, I can't imagine writing on a computer. It'd be like starting all over again as a novelist.

I'm sitting at my desk now. There are several sheets of lined paper staring at me, mocking me, laughing in my face. They're covered with my terrible handwriting. I'm staring back at the lined pages and the terrible handwriting.

The pages are staring right back.

They never blink.

They show me no mercy.

I have a thick folder of ideas somewhere in this office. The cover on the folder is pretty clever. It says IDEAS.

When the time comes for me to consider a new novel, I'll take down the trusty-dusty Idea folder.

I slowly leaf through it, page by page. I usually consider five or six different ideas for each book. I'll flesh out one or two of them.

I live with the idea, go on car rides to nowhere, pondering the idea, trying to shape it into a story I'm excited to work on. Then I start to scribble an outline.

One of the great things about working on several books at the same time is that I've rarely experienced writer's block (except right after Jane died). If a chapter isn't working, I just move on to the next chapter—or I move on to another book.

I know, I know; some writers reading this are rolling their eyes. Or throwing up. What can I tell you? That's what I do. You be you.

When I write a first draft, I try to get the bones of the story down on paper. I don't worry about the language. It's a lot like the way some painters and illustrators work. They do a rough outline, and if they like it, they fill it in, change things, add, delete. I've always felt polishing scenes too early makes it hard to delete them even if they should go. You start thinking, *Oh, I can't throw out that chapter. Oh, I love those two sentences. Oh, man, I love that word choice.*

What you should be thinking is *That doesn't belong in the book, toss it.* When I'm writing a second or third draft, I'll scribble at the top of chapters *Be There.* I'm trying to remind myself to be in the scene, to feel the scene. If I don't feel it, how can I expect the reader to?

name-dropping

that's john updike sitting over there, eating clams

HEY, ONCE UPON a very distant time, long, long ago, I ran into John Updike at a clam shack in Ipswich, Massachusetts. I was just out of grad school, and I was a fan. Actually, I was a John Updike addict and had just read *Rabbit Redux*.

Updike was eating by himself. Small, neat bites, like his sentences. I sat down at a nearby picnic table and watched Updike eat the whole meal. Steamers and a glass of iced tea.

I didn't want to bother him. I just sat there watching. That seemed like enough fun for one afternoon in Ipswich. Man, I loved those Rabbit books of his.

Ipswich wasn't my last time being a celebrity stalker either.

When I was the CEO at J. Walter Thompson North America, three or four times a year we would invite our most important clients to a dinner featuring a guest speaker.

One night we had James Carville and Mary Matalin. That very unlikely husband-and-wife team was funny and engaging and effectively covered both sides of the political aisle. Our agency clients were mostly Republicans, so they loved Mary Matalin, who had been a campaign director for George H. W. Bush. But they had to admit that former Democratic Party consultant Carville was pretty sharp and maybe even funnier than Mary. Maybe, maybe not. Mary doesn't think so.

The following year we invited Tom Wolfe. Actually, I was the one who invited him, and I don't think I've ever heard anybody speak more eloquently than Wolfe. He talked for close to an hour as if he had written out the whole speech, every sentence, polished it, rewritten it, then delivered the talk without a single muff. The words, the sentences, flowed like the best of *The Bonfire of the Vanities* and *The Electric Kool-Aid Acid Test* and *Radical Chic*.

At the end of the evening, I sidled up to Wolfe. "I could give you a ride home. It's right on my way."

That white lie is how I got to be his chauffeur

that night. We arrived in front of his apartment, somewhere on the East Side. We sat in my car and talked for a good half hour. Wolfe was a kind man. Most of the good writers are that way. I try to do the same when I'm approached by people who enjoy my books. My wife, Sue, says that sometimes I'm too kind. But Vonnegut and Tom Wolfe and Wilfrid Sheed were really good role models.

On one of my many book tours, I remember talking with my PR guardian Erinn McGrath about how I was with the public. Erinn said, "Jim, I've been on a lot of tours with a lot of different authors. You aren't just kind to people who like your books or even the ones who don't. You are genuinely interested, warm, patient, and surprisingly open with them." Then Erinn added, "Don't let it go to your head, hotshot."

cruise control

HERE'S HOW I got to meet Tom Cruise.

There was a cover story in the *New York Times Magazine* about me. Tom Cruise read it and called one of his agents at Creative Artists. He wanted to talk to James Patterson.

I happened to be out in LA, and Creative Artists (they're also my agents, though I'm on a much lower rung than Tom Cruise) reached me in my room at the Peninsula. "Tom Cruise wants to meet you." That sounded a little presumptuous, but I was up for it. Then the agent explained the drill.

I was to wait in my room for another phone call. *Okay, I can do that.* I would then be told that Tom Cruise was ready to see me. *Okay, got it.* A town car would be waiting for me outside the Peninsula. *Got it. I'm on my way to the front door. I'm walking fast.* The town-car driver would have an address but I wasn't supposed to tell him who I was going to see. *Cool. So this is like a Tom Cruise adventure movie—like* Mission: Impossible.

I hopped in the town car and was driven to the imposing front gate of a big house somewhere in Beverly Hills. The driver leaned back and said, "Oh, hey, Tom Cruise lives here."

Tom Cruise stood in the driveway to greet me. He had me at *hello*. He and I shared breakfast—really fresh fruit, really crunchy granola, really hot and delicious coffee. His young daughter, Suri, sat in his lap for the whole meal. It was clear that they were very close, and Suri was a doll.

I found Tom to be smart and a total pleasure to talk to. Also, he's not that short. We were together for a good two hours that day. He told me to bring him any projects I thought would be right for him. I never did, but only because I honestly didn't feel I had anything big enough for him. I mean, he wasn't going to be the next Alex Cross. Although in Hollywood, you never know.

Tom walked me out to the town car and he even scribbled down his personal phone number for me.

This is crazy, but I still have it in my wallet.

the stars are out

THIS IS EQUALLY Hollywood-weird: One time, Warren Beatty ambushed me in the outdoor restaurant at the Hotel Bel-Air.

Warren's agent had asked if we—meaning *the agent and I*—could meet. I agreed to that. When we met, the agent told me, in strict confidence, that Warren Beatty might want to talk to me. "Sure," I said. "I'd love to meet Warren Beatty."

The agent shook hands with me and left. Okay. Fine. Less than a minute later, Beatty strolled up to my table, said hello, and sat down. He'd been there in the restaurant the whole time.

We talked for a while, mostly about an idea he had for a mystery film and whether I'd like to collaborate with him. I'd heard (and I don't know if this was true) that Warren had trouble pushing the "go" button on projects, so I told him I wanted to think about it, but eventually I declined. I don't even know if it was a serious offer.

I met with Idris Elba one time in the Roof Garden at the Peninsula Hotel. Idris wanted to play Alex Cross, and I wanted Idris to play Alex. I loved the BBC crime drama *Luther* that he'd starred in for five seasons. Idris is physically imposing. He's also a very funny man.

Jamie Foxx was very interested in playing Alex Cross too (this was well after the two films starring Morgan Freeman). Jamie even agreed to a meeting at Paramount, which is somewhat unusual for a star like him. It's not unusual for writers. Our problem is actually getting a meeting.

Paramount—which owned the rights to Cross—was going through some ups and downs at the time. Jamie and I met with the fourth or fifth different production head they'd had in about a year. This guy was basically a kid, outfitted in a wrinkled T-shirt and ripped jeans, and he seemed pretty full of himself. He asked Jamie, "What would be so different about this new film from our last two Alex Cross films?"

Jamie started to laugh. Then he said, "Do I look like Morgan Freeman to you?"

Then Jamie turned on the charm and I was sure he knew the head of production from somewhere in their Hollywood pasts. When we were leaving Paramount, I asked Jamie about it. He doubled over, laughing. "I never met that squirrelly little fucker in my life."

stories told around amazon's campfire

FOR YEARS, AMAZON hosted writers and other artists at the Campfire, a fall-weekend get-together in Santa Fe, New Mexico. I'd been invited to the Campfire a few times but declined because I didn't feel Amazon always wielded its tremendous power for the good of readers, writers, or publishers. Just my opinion.

Finally, though, I got talked into attending by Larry Kirshbaum, my former publisher at Little, Brown, who had gone to work for Amazon. So Sue and I traveled west to the Campfire.

It was tremendous, actually.

Not once during the three days did the Amazon people talk about their company. I found that impressive as hell. Every day, every hour, was beautifully organized and orchestrated. The mornings consisted of fascinating presentations, possibly modeled on the TED Talks. Every one of them was a hit. Forty-five minutes of nonstop entertainment and information. One example: A British army vet who was the first and only person known to have walked the entire length of the Amazon River. It took him nearly a year—and he was brilliant at describing the nearly impenetrable jungle, the mammal, reptile, and bird life, the creepy insects, and the indigenous people he encountered.

At lunches and dinners, Sue and I were paired with two to four of the other artists. That's how we met actor and bestselling children's author Jamie Lee Curtis—our personal favorite at the Campfire. And the late Sue Grafton, a wonderful Southern charmer. Also Callie Khouri, the gifted screenwriter and producer responsible for the movie *Thelma and Louise* and the TV drama *Nashville*. One night we sat with Lawrence Kasdan, who'd written *The Big Chill* and written and directed *Body Heat*. Unfortunately, Kasdan had attended Michigan, so Sue—a Wisconsin grad—refused to even say hello to him.

Just kidding. They got along great. Everybody gets along with Sue.

I met Jeff Bezos's wife (at the time), MacKenzie Scott. She had gone to prep school at

Hotchkiss (just like our son, Jack), had assisted Toni Morrison in researching her novel *Jazz,* and had written two acclaimed novels of her own. She and her kids were charming, very grounded, and nice to talk to. I even met Jeff Bezos and talked to him briefly. I humbly suggested that Amazon could do a great job getting kids reading—which I told him was a lifesaving exercise. He said he was "on it."

With all due respect to Jeff Bezos, I don't think Amazon has been "on it" when it comes to getting kids reading. Amazon has done many good things, but getting kids reading and loving what they read isn't one of them. There's still time. But maybe not a lot of time. You may have noticed that our country is on fire again. At least part of the reason for that is that so many of our kids can't read.

Think about it for a second. Over half of our country's kids aren't reading at grade level. Amazon could help solve that problem. Why the heck won't they?

tennis, anyone?

ONE OCTOBER, I attended the National Book Festival. On the plane from Florida to Washington, Serena Williams was sitting right behind my bride, Sue, and me. During the flight, half a dozen people came up to Serena and asked for her autograph. She was gracious and polite, which I love.

The flight landed, and Sue and I stood up and started to hoist our bags out of the overhead.

Serena stepped up close to me and said in a low voice (which I can still hear today), "They want my autograph, but I want yours."

Well, I turned a bright shade of red. I loved the compliment, but I couldn't believe Serena Williams was talking to me. Even better, she said she liked my books.

Sue, Serena, and I walked together to baggage

claim. Serena kept saying, "I can't believe you're James Patterson."

I came back with "I can't believe you're Serena Williams." It was a nice, funny, very human moment for the three of us. It showed that Serena and I could laugh at ourselves.

The night before the National Mall filled with tens of thousands of readers gathered to hear from poets, authors, and storytellers, I entered the Jefferson Building inside the Library of Congress to attend the fundraising gala. The late Tom Clancy was the dinner speaker. Tom was a very successful thriller writer, but his speech in the Coolidge Auditorium that night was not all that thrilling.

While dessert was being served, Sue went wandering off. She ran into First Lady Laura Bush, former teacher and librarian and host of the gala and festival. She came back to our table and said, "The president wants to see you. Get your butt over there."

So I wandered over to meet George W. Bush for the first time. I was kind of surprised that I could walk right up to his table. No wanding, no pat-downs.

President Bush and I stood there chatting a little bit. I liked him right away, and I'm not even a Republican. He said, "Jim, I hear you're pretty good at speeches."

"Well, not as good as you," I said, and I should have stopped right there. But I went on. "I might've done a little better than Tom did tonight."

As I was saying what I shouldn't have been saying, Tom Clancy came walking up behind W. I don't know how the president saw Clancy, but he was quick on his feet. Suddenly he said, "Oh, hey, Tom, Jim was just saying what a great job you did tonight."

President Bush covered for me. W. turned out to be an excellent wingman.

texas-style

I TRY MY best not to get political, especially when I'm interviewed on television. I'm not comfortable broadcasting my political or socioeconomic opinions, and I usually get itchy and twitchy watching other writers or actors getting up on soapboxes they don't always deserve to be standing on. I don't believe everything in life comes down to politics, but sometimes I feel like I'm one of the very few people thinking that way. I guess I consider myself an Independent. I definitely want to hear what everybody has to say, both sides of the argument.

Anyway, in 2004, the Bushes invited Sue and me to Fort Worth for the fifteenth anniversary of Barbara's Foundation for Family Literacy. The program was driven by Mrs. Bush's belief that "the home is a child's first school, the parent is a child's first teacher, and reading is a child's first subject."

Let your children see you read.

Sue and I spent the day with George H. W. and Barbara. David Halberstam was there and we talked about *The Best and the Brightest,* his narrative of America's involvement in Vietnam that the *Boston Globe* had likened to "watching an Alfred Hitchcock thriller," and about his time in Moscow. The novelist Daniel Silva was also at the Bushes'. I'm a fan of Silva's wonderfully complex Israeli hero, or maybe antihero, Gabriel Allon. Silva can really write. The bastard.

While we were at the Bush apartment, Barbara pretty much ran the show. But every once in a while President Bush would sneak her a look that communicated *Okay, enough. Let's not forget I was president.* And Barbara would give him a look that seemed to say *Heard that one before.*

I found the Bushes to be down-to-earth and they both had a terrific sense of humor. When some people get a little too over-the-top negative about Bill and Hillary Clinton, I'll say to them, "You respect the Bushes, right?" If they're being honest, most will admit, "Yeah,

yeah, the Bushes are good people." Then I come back with "Well, the Bushes love the Clintons. So that's got to tell you something about the Clintons." The two families were close, especially President Clinton and 41.

It seems to me there's a nasty little disease going around and it's especially prevalent on TV and radio news shows. It goes something like this: "My view of the world is right—and your view is stupid!" I really don't like that. Honestly, it makes me a little sick to my stomach.

Do I believe Al Franken should have had his Senate career ruined? My personal opinion—no. Do I know what went on between Woody Allen and the Farrows? Nope. And neither do you. And neither did the Hachette Book Group employees, none of whom had read Allen's autobiography *Apropos of Nothing*, when they demanded the publisher not publish it. Maybe I'm hopelessly old-fashioned, but I'm almost always on the side of free speech.

the power of stories,
and john grisham

I'VE GIVEN TEN college-commencement speeches. I change the content each time but a theme I love is the power of stories. I have honorary doctorates from the University of Florida, University of the Pacific, University of Arkansas, Montclair State University, Florida Atlantic University, and Wisconsin.

So if we ever happen to meet, I'm "Dr. Dr. Dr. Dr. Dr. Dr. Patterson." Sounds like I belong in a Joseph Heller novel.

The Mississippi State graduation turned out to be a particularly memorable ceremony. Nice, nice people, and, Lord, were they hospitable. They provided Sue and me with a house on campus and candy in all the little crystal bowls.

John Grisham received his undergraduate degree at Mississippi State before he went to the University of Mississippi for law school. I called Grisham up and said, "Hey, I'm going to be giving the commencement speech at one of your alma maters. How about we do a benefit for kids' books at a local bookstore or library?"

John, who writes books for kids too, said, "That'd be great, I'm in." He asked me for the date of the graduation. I told him and he said, "My wife and I are going to be in Paris then."

We talked for another few minutes and near the end of the call I said, "I hope you and your wife have a great time in Paris."

Grisham had the last word and a pretty funny line. "And you have a great time in *Starkville, Mississippi.*"

That I did.

collaborating with president clinton

BILL CLINTON AND I have the same wise and talented lawyer and friend, Bob Barnett, who also serves as our literary agent (although Bob hates being called an agent, and who could blame him). Bob is there for President Clinton, and he's there for me, 24/7. That goes for all of his clients, even slackers like Bob Woodward and Jake Tapper.

Here's what I mean when I say Bob is there for us 24/7. He came over to our house in Florida one night for dinner. (Actually, he's a moocher and has come over several times.) By the end of the meal, he had seventy-four texts backed up on his phone.

Bob is much more than a hard worker. He is so persuasive and persistent and charming that he got President Clinton and me to consider writing a suspense novel together and then to actually do the deed.

The result was *The President Is Missing,* which became the bestselling novel of 2018. Bob was right.

Then Mr. Barnett was right a second time. He badgered (Bob attended Wisconsin as an undergraduate) the president and me into writing a second thriller. This turned out to be *The President's Daughter,* which was also a number 1 bestseller. I think it's an even better story than our first collaboration. Maybe President Clinton and I are improving with age. Well, maybe not.

When Bill Clinton and I were writing our books, the president would call me every once in a while. I found it very cool to be getting calls, sometimes late in the night, from a former president.

I gave President Clinton a couple of beer mugs for his most recent birthday. One of the mugs was inscribed THE PRESIDENT IS DRINKING, a play on our bestseller *The President Is Missing.* The other was inscribed YOU'RE ONLY OLD ONCE. BOTTOMS UP. I'll drink to that.

One time he had to give his Georgetown fiftieth-reunion speech and he wanted my reaction. He was nervous about the speech, which is interesting for somebody who's given some relatively important speeches around the world.

There was a paragraph in the speech to his Georgetown classmates that I particularly loved. President Clinton wrote, "We can't give in to the current craze to demean and debase, to leave no insult unhurled, no stone unthrown. We just can't quit or criticize, because we're old enough to remember another time of great struggle over whether our differences are more important than our common humanity, whether conflict is more important than cooperation. Whether subtraction and division will chase away our children's and grandchildren's dreams before we rediscover the virtues of addition and multiplication."

The man can write. No wonder I picked him to be my cowriter.

Oh, yeah, I forgot—he picked me.

golfing with presidents

I'VE PLAYED GOLF with three presidents—41, 42, and 45.

George Bush Senior, 41, ran around the course like the Energizer Bunny. He seemed to have a really good time doing it. George H. W. was a movie-superhero blur out there.

President Clinton and I have played four or five rounds and it's always been a blast. When we're together, it's just two hackers messing around. We'll hit extra balls, occasionally land some really good shots and some bad ones. It's never serious when we play. No ten-dollar bets. An occasional mulligan.

The two of us were photographed repeatedly on the course during an interview for *Sports Illustrated.* I tried to set the tone of the story for the writer, Jack McCallum. President Clinton and I were just going to go out there and have some fun. No scorecards.

McCallum wanted to cause some trouble, of course. That's what he's supposed to do. It's his job. So he asked which one of us was the better golfer. I told him, "Well, President Clinton is faster giving a four-foot putt. I'm faster dropping a second ball after a bad shot."

On we went to the first hole, a par five.

I hate to admit this in print, but I muffed my second shot into the rough. Just to be sure I had made my point with McCallum, I yelled over to him, "Hey, make yourself useful, Jack. Pick up that stray ball for me." Fortunately, he thought that was pretty funny. Then I showed him how quickly I could drop a second ball.

I've also played with President Trump. So has President Clinton. Donald Trump is a serious golfer, easily the best golfer of the presidents I've played with. He's somewhere between a four and six handicapper. For real. And I have no reason to make that up.

Before Donald Trump was president and before I had collaborated with President Clinton on a novel, I took two friends of mine to play at Trump National in Westchester. My friends and I had grown up together in Newburgh and I figured it would be a story for them just to be on one of Trump's courses.

So, we're playing the third or fourth hole, and one of my friends looks over to the sixth hole. His eyes go wide. "Is that Donald Trump? Is that President Clinton?"

Yes, it was. Trump and Clinton were playing golf together, which is its own interesting piece of history. It's the way things used to be in politics, though. Better, saner times.

My friends and I finished our round and got to the clubhouse just as Donald Trump and President Clinton were getting up from lunch.

We started walking across the dining room and President Clinton was staring at me. Normally, I wouldn't have bothered him, but I said, "Hi, I'm Jim Patterson."

Clinton said, "Oh, I know who you are. I recognized you right away."

I said, "Well, I recognized you too."

At that point, my buddies, Bob Hatfield and Mike Smith, who were both card-carrying Republicans, asked if they could take a picture with President Clinton. I decided it would be another great story for them to bring home to Newburgh, but I would sit this one out.

I hunkered down at a dining table and watched them do some mischief out on the lawn. Melania took a photograph of my friends with President Clinton.

Then I watched them shaking Donald Trump's hand. I knew he didn't like to shake hands. When they got back to the table, I asked, "What was going on with Donald Trump out there?"

My friend Bobby Hatfield said, "We told him we played basketball against him in high school." This was true enough. Donald Trump went to New York Military Academy, which is located not far from Newburgh. Our schools had played against one another. Trump said to my friends, "I hope we won."

Hatfield said, "Nah, we kicked your ass." Both Donald Trump and President Clinton got a laugh out of that one. What an image. Donald Trump and Bill Clinton enjoying a good laugh together.

One more story.

In the fall of 2019, Little, Brown was contacted and told I was being considered for either the National Humanities Medal or a National Medal of Arts. In the past, the National Medal of Arts had been awarded to my old lunch pal John Updike, Toni Morrison, Joan Didion, August Wilson, Philip Roth. My publisher was informed that I might get a call from the White House.

The call came one Friday while I was working in my home office. A very official-sounding male on the line said, "Please hold for the president."

I couldn't resist and I said, "Which president?"

The award ceremony at the White House was very gracious and memorable for Sue and me and the Little, Brown people.

you called the president *what?*

AS I SAID earlier, President Clinton and I have played golf together a few times. Of course, there had to be a first time. When you're with a former president, you have to feel your way. What we've evolved to is that when we are in public together, everything is appropriately respectful—*Mr. President this, Mr. President that*—but in private, we're just two guys.

Up to a point. Hell, the man had been the most powerful person on the planet. You don't get over that. I guess. How would I know? I'm not even the most powerful person in my house.

The first time we went golfing, Tina Flournoy, President Clinton's brilliant chief of staff (she's now Vice President Kamala Harris's chief of staff), told me, "The president will only play nine holes." I'm like, *That's fine. It's cool. I'm*

okay if he only wants to play one hole. Or we could
have a putting contest on the practice green.

So we played. He drove the golf cart—and think about it, Bill Clinton has driven a car like twice in the last twenty years. He's dangerous on the cart paths. Pedal to the metal even flying down steep hills, on the *sides* of hills, skirting streams and ponds, crossing a highway where real cars go real fast.

Anyway, on the fourth or fifth hole, he had a putt for birdie. It was a short putt, maybe eight feet. He left it three feet short.

Now, if you play golf, you know you just don't leave a birdie putt short. And definitely not three feet short. And that's why a word came out of my mouth that I never expected to say to a president. "You [the word I never expected to say to a president]!" President Clinton said, "Did you just call me a [the word I never expected to say to a president]?" I nodded. Then he said, "Well, you're right, I am a [the word I never expected a president to say]."

And that mildly blue exchange sort of set the tone for us. When nobody's around, we're just two human beings.

That first nine we played turned into eighteen holes. He was enjoying himself. So was I.

Around the twelfth hole, Hillary called. She was off on a book tour. The president told her, "Oh, I'm out here with Jim. We're having a great time. We're like two high-school boys playing hooky."

He and Hillary talked for about five minutes and at the end of the call, he said, "I love you." I don't think a lot of people expect that Bill and Hillary are like that. Those people couldn't be more wrong.

The first time my wife, Sue, and I went out to dinner with them, we noticed that two or three times during the meal they were holding hands under the table. What can I say—I love that.

It reminds me of the way I am with Sue. Every night—and I mean *every night*—she and I go to sleep holding hands.

the tv camera doesn't like writers much

THE MORNING TV shows are pretty good about interviewing authors, God bless them. Unfortunately a lot of TV hosts, as well as print and online journalists, don't like to interview writers, with the exception of authors of topical, usually controversial political nonfiction. I don't completely blame the journalists. To properly prepare, they have to read an entire book. That's a tough ask. Also, a lot of writers are deadly on TV. They go on and on until it's time for the blessed relief of a pharmaceutical or insurance commercial.

The nicest reporters—to me—are Al Roker, Hoda Kotb, and Gayle King. They ask smart questions and they're not there to make themselves look good. They're fair. They like books and they read a lot.

Matt Lauer conducted one of the best

interviews and then, later, one of the worst interviews I've ever had. Early on, I did a twenty-minute segment with him on CNBC. He asked thoughtful questions, listened to the answers, then asked smart follow-up questions. That's rare on television, trust me. On the other hand, one time on the *Today* show, he read a couple of generic lines about Alex Cross—something like "Alex Cross walked along M Street in Georgetown," blah-blah-blah—then asked me which of my Alex Cross novels the totally nondescript passage had come from. To his credit, Matt apologized at the end of the segment.

During the book tour with President Clinton, I appeared early one morning on *Squawk Box*. I like the show and I like the hosts. But occasionally they have a guest host and that morning it was Ken Langone, who was one of the founders of Home Depot.

I sat down next to Langone. We were twenty seconds from the end of a commercial break, about to go on live.

He leaned in close and said, "Why would you write a book with that bum Bill Clinton?"

I couldn't believe what I was hearing. So here's what I said to Langone, who is a big donor to NYU's hospitals; the NYU Langone Medical

Center is named for him and his wife. "Ken, if you go there during our interview, I'm going to talk on national TV about what a bad experience I had at the Langone Medical Center."

Langone never said one word during the interview. The other *Squawk Box* hosts took over.

When the segment was done, Langone leaned in close again. "What happened to you at my hospital?"

I told him, "Ken, I was never at your hospital. Have a nice day."

just another idiot wandering planet earth

THIS IS THE last famous name I'll drop. (I probably won't keep that promise.)

I saw Bruce Springsteen on Broadway. I was watching the Boss from the audience. Not even good seats. I've never been somebody who likes to use whatever celebrity status I might have to go backstage after a show or down onto a football field at halftime or into some basketball team's smelly locker room before the game.

Up onstage that night, Springsteen talked about being something of a fraud because he pretended that he was somebody he really wasn't. He felt that he hadn't really lived the life described in his songs. They were fiction. Just poetry. (Really good poetry, though.)

My entire life, I honestly have had no idea who the hell I am. It's still that way.

I look at myself as just another idiot wandering

planet Earth with no real idea what makes the world go 'round, no particular identity, just another lost soul.

Like the Boss that night on Broadway.

I still have dreams, of course. For example, I dream about being nominated for the Nobel Prize in Literature.

In the dream I arrive in Stockholm for the award ceremony on December 10. I get all the way to the front door of the Stockholm Concert Hall.

At the door, the judges are assembled to greet me.

They're all there waiting.

Smiling big Swedish smiles.

And they say, in unison, "*Gotcha!* You're not going to win the Nobel Prize, James. Not going to happen. Not on our watch."

still a hungry dog

hollywood called

I'M A BIG fan of the Randy Newman song "I Love L.A." and the entire politically incorrect, deliciously subversive album *Trouble in Paradise*. As for Hollywood, I guess I have mixed feelings. One of the jokes I tell is that somewhere along the way, Hollywood called—and I made the rookie mistake of answering.

At its heart, the film business is pretty straightforward and easy to understand: agents and producers, directors and stars—but especially agents—go where the money is. If you're hot, they're there for you. You can't really blame them. It's show *business,* right?

I've had a few agents, but mostly I've been represented by Creative Artists. Once, two agents from a rival agency asked me to lunch at Le Bernardin in Manhattan. It was a strange meeting, because when I eat, I eat (especially at Le Bernardin). When I do business, I do business. Up to a point.

During the meal, these agents never said a word about why they or their agency would be a good fit for me, how they felt about my books, nothing of substance. Also, nothing very funny or interesting. I swear, our waiter at Le Bernardin was a better lunch companion than these two.

Finally, I felt compelled to ask the agents, "This is probably a stupid question, but what separates you from CAA or other agencies? I mean—for a novelist? For me?"

The agents gave me an honest answer that I found pretty damn funny. One of them said, "James, here's how we're different from the other agencies—we actually *read the books*."

I liked the line so much, I picked up the check.

hollywood shorts

WHEN I FINISHED *Along Came a Spider*—the first Alex Cross book—we got a big offer from one of the Hollywood studios. They loved the book, loved Alex Cross, and only wanted one small change—they wanted me to rewrite Cross as a white man. That was not happening. Not for seven figures. Not ever. And at the time of the offer, I didn't have much money in the bank.

Bill Robinson runs my film and TV business, along with Patrick Santa and Max DiLallo. Bill went to Brown University, just like my son, Jack. Actually, Bill and Jack are somewhat Brown-obsessed.

On the subject of Brown, one time I spent the better part of a day with CNN's legal expert Jeffrey Toobin. Toobin went to Harvard, but one of his sons went to Brown. I asked him if the son enjoyed it. "Yes, he loved it!" Then Toobin smiled. "Of course, I don't consider Brown a university. I consider it a cult." Bill Robinson and Jack would agree, since they're card-carrying cult members.

I've met my share of movie stars. People ask incredibly goofy questions about them. Like *Who's better-looking, Hugh Jackman or Charlize Theron?* Actually, they both look amazing in real life. Also, they don't seem full of themselves. Oh, and Charlize is better-looking. From my perspective, anyway.

I was invited to the writers' room during preproduction of the CBS series based on my books *Zoo* and *Instinct*. As you might know, I get slapped around a little about cowriting.

Let me set the scene inside a typical network-TV-series writers' room. Six to ten writers basically *cowrite* the forty-three-minute scripts. Usually there are notes and story ideas plastered all over the walls. Who says writing has to be a lonely profession?

When I came to visit, the TV writers were nice enough and we had some laughs. But I'll never forget an exchange with the writing team for *Zoo*. One of the showrunners said, "Listen, let's be honest here, James—the novel *Zoo* is a B-level thriller. But trust me, we're going to make an A-level TV series."

Yep, that's what he said. Now, let me be honest. *Zoo* wasn't an A-level TV series either. I always felt that *Zoo* needed to be a feature film because the special effects would be silly, or at least unconvincing, on a network-TV budget.

They were.

Just being honest.

One last Hollywood story. Barbara Hall, the showrunner on *Madam Secretary*, wrote a terrific pilot and series outline based on my nonfiction book *The House of Kennedy*. Barbara's pilot had some fine writing and storytelling about America's royal family. One of the head honchos at the network involved killed the project. He said, "It's mainly about rich white guys, and I'm a white guy, and I don't feel comfortable green-lighting it." I get it, but so much for fifty years of history and the Kennedy family. So much for John and Bobby Kennedy, just two rich white guys who happened to die for their country. You gotta love Hollywood.

alex cross goes hollywood

WAY BACK WHEN it was politically and socially correct (before the sultan of Brunei bought the place), I used to stay at the gorgeous Hotel Bel-Air in Los Angeles. Not that it really matters, but back in the day, so did Michelle and Barack Obama.

I was heading into the restaurant at the Bel-Air late one night just when producers David Brown and Joe Wizan were leaving. They greeted me warmly. Years before, David and Joe had optioned my book *The Midnight Club* and sworn they were going to get it made.

That didn't happen, although it got close, with Sylvester Stallone set to play the lead. But I liked Joe and David. Joe, who had once run 20th Century Fox, grinned and asked, "What are you working on now? Or are you *resting on your laurel?*"

"I'm still waiting for that first laurel, Joe, but I do have a new book I like."

"Do tell," said David Brown.

I told Joe and David about a smart, charismatic African-American detective named Alex Cross. I had just finished the second Cross novel, *Kiss the Girls,* and I spun the plot right there on the restaurant steps. The classic Hollywood elevator pitch, without the elevator, delivered in under two minutes.

Joe and David said, almost in one voice, "You've got to send it to us. Send it *tomorrow.* We'll read it before end of day."

I knew that probably meant some recent Stanford or USC grad would read *Kiss the Girls* sometime that month, but I sent Joe and David the book. I didn't expect anything would come of it. It's not unusual in Hollywood to get gushy enthusiasm for material *before* it gets read, and if it's a novel, that typically means never.

But two days later, not only had David and Joe read *Kiss the Girls,* they'd bought it.

Next came the real miracle. Paramount got involved and it looked like the movie was actually going to be made. Morgan Freeman had agreed to play Alex Cross. We had a hot young director named Gary Fleder.

Now, I had been on set for a lot of commercials, but I'd never been on a big Hollywood studio's movie set before. We were shooting in North Carolina. Everybody was super-polite to me. But I soon found out that on the movie set, the novelist rates somewhere below the caterer. *They know why the caterer is there.*

Ashley Judd was one of the leads in *Kiss the Girls*. She had left the University of Kentucky to start a career in films and she was smart and funny. A lot of *Kiss the Girls* was shot in the thick, buggy woods, and Ashley started calling it *Kiss the Squirrels.*

On the first day of shooting, Paramount still hadn't cast one of the two villains. I was used to running buttoned-up commercial shoots at J. Walter Thompson, and I found the situation on *Kiss the Girls,* frankly, unbelievable. There were scenes with the villain later that week—and they hadn't even cast the part.

That night I had dinner with David and Joe. They could see that I was agitated. David was an avuncular, college-professor type and very experienced in the film world. He'd run Paramount at one point. He proceeded to tell me that on a movie set, "The director is the pilot.

Once you start shooting, you have to let the pilot fly the plane."

I listened politely and nodded like I was ten years old, but I knew it was just more Hollywood bullshit. And David Brown, whom I respected, could shovel shit with the best of them.

I also knew that Paramount had sent a casting selection for the villain to the director, Gary Fleder. They wanted to hire Cary Elwes for the part. I thought Elwes was a fine choice.

At nine that night, Fleder still hadn't even looked at the tape. Suddenly, Joe and David got up from the dinner table. They left me drinking my coffee and rushed off to the shoot to make the director look at the damn casting tape.

I sat at the table by myself, thinking, *So much for letting the director fly the plane.*

the book is always better than the movie (except for *the godfather*, and maybe *goodfellas*—oh, yeah, and *forrest gump*)

HERE'S THE OPENING line for a Hollywood novel I'll never write: "Hello, I lied."

Studios often arrange expensive press junkets to promote their new releases, and Paramount invited me to the junket for *Along Came a Spider*. One of the studio's PR people showed me the film because Paramount knew the press would ask me about it. (In case you're confused, *Along Came a Spider* was published before *Kiss the Girls,* but *Kiss the Girls* was the first movie made.)

I watched the first scene and thought, *That wasn't in the book.* I watched the second scene.... *That wasn't in the book either.* In the third scene, Alex Cross is building a ship in a bottle.... *That doesn't seem very cinematic to me.* A woman appears and tells Alex, *Enough with* the ships-in-a-bottle, why don't you go out and shoot somebody? Or at least get shot at.

Now, I had *no idea* who the woman in the movie scene was, and *I wrote the book.*

Later in the glitzy press junket, I ran into Morgan Freeman. He was always nice to me, but I think he's nice to everybody. I asked Morgan who the woman in the third scene of the movie was.

In his unmistakable Voice of God, Morgan told me the woman was Alex Cross's *sister.*

I said, "Oh...*I didn't know Alex had a sister!*"

Years later, when we were shooting the movie *Along Came a Spider* in Washington, DC, I got to go to dinner with Morgan, producer Joe Wizan, his lovely wife, and my equally lovely wife, Sue.

We ate in a little Italian restaurant. When we were getting up from the table, Clint Eastwood and *Law and Order* star and former Tennessee senator Fred Thompson came by to say hello. Now, Morgan, Eastwood, and Thompson were all over six foot three. People around the little restaurant were starting to watch us.

One man actually rose from his table and approached us. He said he wanted an autograph.

My autograph.

Clint Eastwood looked down at the guy and cracked, "I need a hit movie...*bad.*"

the president is missing, hollywood-style

THE PRESIDENT IS MISSING, the first novel I wrote with Bill Clinton, got a lot of press—some of it a bit painful. (Not the reviews, which were stellar, among the best I've ever gotten.)

Here's what happened. The president and I did a taped interview for the *Today* show. Craig Melvin "hosted the roast." NBC had promised it would only deal with the novel, but that isn't what happened—and to be fair, it's kind of the way a lot of journalism works. The president and I knew that going in.

Now, my job, I swear, was to keep the president on topic—the topic being our novel *The President Is Missing*. He wasn't accustomed to the four-minute clips that novelists typically get on TV. Four minutes goes by like snapping your fingers twice.

Almost before the director called out, "Action,"

Craig Melvin launched into the subject of the #MeToo movement. The president and I were prepared—but Melvin took a different tack. He asked President Clinton why he had never apologized to Monica Lewinsky. Well, obviously he had—multiple times. I'd seen it on national TV. The question upset the president—as I thought it should.

He and Melvin were *off*—and definitely off the topic of *The President Is Missing.*

Now, since I was the president's wingman, I was trying to figure out how to stop this in mid-mess.

My first thought—which I instantly vetoed—was to ask Craig Melvin if he wanted to talk about #MeToo using a more recent example, like NBC's own Matt Lauer's troubles. I hated that idea and I knew the president would hate it too.

Next, I considered standing up from my chair, saying, "Time for a Coca-Cola break," and walking directly in front of the cameras. Not only would that stop the melee, but because I used a product name, they probably wouldn't use the bite anywhere. Finally, I asked Craig Melvin if he wanted to go even farther back in history on the subject of presidents and #MeToo issues. Lyndon Johnson? John Kennedy? FDR? How about Thomas Jefferson? That worked, but the damage had been done.

I will never forget how nasty, how downright cruel it got during that book tour. I felt like I was in the middle of a firefight. Nobody was actually shooting at me—but it was still depressing and terrifying to be there as an unwilling eyewitness.

I'll do my best to describe the two days of meetings the president and I had in Hollywood trying to decide who would get the screen rights to *The President Is Missing*.

Seventeen prospective buyers showed up. We met with them in a penthouse suite at the Beverly Wilshire Hotel. They ranged from private investors to movie studios to streaming services and even a few top directors. To put that in perspective, what usually happens when I send a new novel to Hollywood is it goes from an assistant to the assistant's junk e-mail. I wish I was kidding. That's what happens to most books, though.

So President Clinton and I listened to seventeen feverish pitches over the course of two days. He liked the attention, but I loved it.

Of course, nobody had actually read our book. But they'd read a nine-page synopsis and now here they were with their checkbooks out.

And they bid. About half of the seventeen were all in. A few dropped out after one investor group came in with a high-seven-figure bid on day one. These two young cocks told us to take it or leave it—*on the spot.* We called their bluff—on the spot—and they stayed in the bidding anyway.

At the end of the two days, Showtime made the best bid. A really, really good bid. We took it. On the spot.

There's one funny story about that trip to LA.

President Clinton and I stayed at the Beverly Wilshire Hotel. The Secret Service liked the place and felt it was easier to provide protection there than at other hotels. When I arrived, I went up to the front desk to check in. There was some kind of misunderstanding.

I was asked, very politely, if I would take a seat in the lobby. It would just be a minute. They needed to clear something up.

About five minutes later, two Secret Service agents showed up in the lobby. They were part of President Clinton's detail and I knew them.

They apologized to me for the confusion. Then they assured the front-desk person that I was indeed the writer James Patterson.

I found out later what had happened.

There's another James Patterson who lives in Palm Beach. We're friendly. He used to own Long John Silver's. Sometimes when he travels and checks in at a nice hotel like the Beverly Wilshire, he's asked if he's me. And sometimes he says, "Yes, I'm *the* James Patterson." Occasionally, that gets him an upgrade or maybe some extra fruit.

It turns out *that* James Patterson stays at the Beverly Wilshire when he's in LA. So they knew *that* James Patterson as the writer James Patterson.

When I arrived—and because President Clinton was staying there—the hotel staff assumed I wasn't me and that put them on red alert. They called for the Secret Service.

Because of all the confusion and embarrassment at the front desk, I was the James Patterson who got the upgrade this time. And some extra fruit.

murder of a small town

MY JOURNALIST FRIEND Tim Malloy and I wrote and self-produced a documentary called *Murder of a Small Town*. Our hope was to draw some positive attention to Belle Glade and Pahokee, Florida, in the western part of Palm Beach County, as well as to my hometown, Newburgh, New York. The film turned out to be an emotional indictment of racial injustice. We finished it in 2014.

When people think about Palm Beach County, they imagine it's all like the town of Palm Beach—incredible wealth, gated estates, sandy beaches, Tiffany and Hermès boutiques, and, of course, Mar-a-Lago.

That isn't even close to the truth. Palm Beach County is actually the largest agricultural county in Florida—and the far western part is very poor and can be violent.

When Tim and I made the film, Newburgh

was ranked the sixth-most-violent small town in America. Belle Glade was ranked first. But both towns were filled with good people, a lot of whom couldn't get jobs. If we could, we wanted to do the right thing by Belle Glade and Newburgh.

I tend to be obsessive about efficiency and tight budget controls. It's a hang-up that probably goes all the way back to the days I was growing up without much money in Newburgh. It's definitely the way it was when I was running J. Walter Thompson North America. This film was a good example of how efficiency can work and help get more projects done.

We bid the film out to two top documentary companies, one in New York, one in LA. Both came in with bids over $700,000. Tim and I thought the bids were outrageously high. Absurd. Dumb. As a TV news journalist, Tim had shot a lot of film. I had produced movies, TV shows, and thousands of TV commercials. We knew we could do *Murder of a Small Town* for a lot less.

That's what we did. We finished the film, all in, for $51,000. We shot it with a local cameraman. Then Tim and I edited it in a strip mall in West Palm.

The documentary went on to win two 2016 Emmys and appeared on PBS and Netflix. So much for $700,000 productions.

Most important, the documentary helped people understand what can happen to a small town, what *is* happening to small towns all over the country. Obviously, people are suffering; some have given up hope, way too many are turning to life-threatening—sometimes life-ending—drugs.

Again and again, strangers came up to Tim and me. They said that *Murder of a Small Town* helped them to understand and frequently made them cry. It helped them see that towns like Belle Glade and Pahokee, Florida, and Newburgh, New York, are filled with good people, people who sometimes also need a little help to get moving in the right direction. Just a little push. That's all it takes sometimes.

to tell the truth

THE FIRST NONFICTION narrative I ever wanted to write was *Filthy Rich,* the story of serial predator Jeffrey Epstein. That raises an interesting question—why do I choose certain stories over others?

Let's stay with that piece of human garbage, Jeffrey Epstein. Why did I want to write his story?

In 2015, I was having a couple of beers with Tim Malloy at the Palm Beach Grill. He was telling me about an unbelievable local news story he'd covered in 2008—Jeffrey Epstein's "catch and release" tale. I wasn't familiar with Epstein back then. Most people outside Florida weren't.

But Tim had me hooked. I found Epstein's story to be a mind-exploder—and that's why I decided to write about it, with help from Tim and a fine New York journalist named John

Connolly. If you don't already know it, here's the story: A billionaire living part-time in Palm Beach has sex with literally hundreds of underage girls. The Palm Beach police get a dozen of these girls to make statements and do filmed interviews. Epstein is toast. He's going away forever. But then he gets a sweetheart deal and only serves eleven months in a cushy county jail in West Palm Beach. He's even permitted to leave jail and go to his office weekdays between nine and six.

In 2016, when the book *Filthy Rich* was about to be published, I took it to CNN, Fox News, all the networks. Not one of them felt that Jeffrey Epstein was important or newsworthy enough to cover the story. Not one of them was interested in the victimized girls. Unbelievable as that sounds, it's what happened in 2016. Another detail that never got reported: when I was writing the book, Epstein's lawyers threatened legal action against me every other week.

This gets even crazier. In 2019, three years after *Filthy Rich* was published, the *Miami Herald* ran a fine series of articles on Epstein. But something else had happened that put even more spin on the story. R. Alexander Acosta had been the federal prosecutor who agreed to the sweetheart deal for Epstein. In 2017, Acosta was appointed secretary of labor by President Trump.

Bingo!

Suddenly, the Epstein story was a rocket ship. In 2016, nobody in the press seemed to care much about Epstein or the abused girls, the victims. Apparently, the girls, some of them as young as fourteen, weren't newsworthy. But now, Jeffrey Epstein was on every front page and all over the airwaves because of the Acosta and Trump connection.

In May of 2020, the documentary inspired by the book ran as a four-part series on Netflix—*Jeffrey Epstein: Filthy Rich*. It was a tough film to watch but it was number 1 in the U.S., and Netflix estimated that over a hundred million people saw it around the world.

Tim Malloy, John Connolly, and I celebrated sharing at least a small part in bringing Jeffrey Epstein down. It was a good thing to do but it should've happened years, if not a decade, earlier.

I don't have much interest in telling Ghislaine Maxwell's story, not in book form, anyway, but if I did, I think I came up with a fitting title for Epstein's girl-pal—*Filthy Bitch*.

you can't make this stuff up

HERE'S THE BASICALLY unsolvable problem I have with writing nonfiction.

I have a big, sprawling, way overheated imagination, but you aren't supposed to make stuff up in nonfiction. Of course, writers do it all the time. If you have any doubts about that, listen to this: There are over two hundred books about William Shakespeare. Here's the interesting plot twist that Bill Bryson points out in *Shakespeare: The World As Stage*. Other than the plays that Shakespeare wrote, virtually nothing is known about the Bard. *Nothing*. And yet there have been all of these scholarly works about Shakespeare's life. So what are they—*fiction?*

When I decided to write more nonfiction, I wanted to do it differently than most of the weighty tomes I read and then use as doorstops. I suspect that a lot of people don't read much nonfiction because so many of these books tell more than we want to know. A whole lot more. Nine hundred fifty-nine pages on Ulysses S. Grant? (Now, I happened to love Ron Chernow's book on Grant, but for some readers there might be too many facts, too much information, and, maybe, not enough story.)

I wanted to write nonfiction as involving *stories*. More like fiction. Books that would be hard to put down rather than difficult to finish. Closer to Laura Hillenbrand's *Unbroken* than William Manchester's *The Last Lion*.

After I finished *Filthy Rich*, I started *All-American Murder*, about the homicidal pro football player Aaron Hernandez. It was another complex, twisted story I couldn't resist. I even did the on-camera interviews for the special about Hernandez that ran on *48 Hours*. I got to work with the great Susan Zirinsky on the project, as well as the talented producer Jamie Stolz.

When I was doing the interviews for *48 Hours*, I knew I was supposed to act like Anderson Cooper or Lesley Stahl or Scott Pelley. But I just couldn't do it.

At one point, I'm up in Boston talking with Ursula Ward, the mother of Odin Lloyd, who was murdered by Hernandez. And as I listened to Ursula's sad story, I'm crying. *I'm crying on camera*.

So much for my budding career as a serious, objective TV journalist. And yet Susan Zirinsky said I could work on *48 Hours* anytime I needed a little extra cash.

I cowrote *The House of Kennedy* because I felt the Kennedy saga was the most powerful family story in American history. The Kennedys *are* America's royal family. This is America's *Crown*, except that several of the Kennedys are more rounded and interesting characters than Queen Elizabeth was in *The Crown*.

I decided to do *The Last Days of John Lennon* for a lot of very personal reasons. I was living on Central Park West, just a few blocks from the Dakota, when John Lennon was shot and murdered there. I was part of the crowd that gathered outside the Dakota after Lennon died. The famous photo that my friend Harry Benson took—the grieving crowd in Central Park with someone holding a sign that says WHY?—is hanging right here in my office. Maybe the weirdest thing: our home in Palm Beach is connected by a twenty-foot-long bridge to the house Yoko Ono and John Lennon bought in 1980, the last year of his life.

But most important, I loved Lennon's music, during and after his time as a Beatle, and the way he tried to use it to make the world a little better place.

Imagine that.

I decided on *The Defense Lawyer* because I felt Barry Slotnick's story was wonderfully perverse and controversial but most of all because Slotnick was always honest about his personal beliefs. He defended John Gotti, Joe Colombo, the subway shooter Bernie Goetz—and during one twelve-year stretch in his career, Barry Slotnick never lost a case. As a storyteller, I was *in*. Barry is a great character who believes that everybody has a right to be represented in court.

So now I'm hooked on writing nonfiction. And I haven't gone over five hundred pages yet. I just tell stories and I don't even have to make anything up. Almost seems too easy.

a letter to the *new york times*

IN EARLY 2019, I started work on a nonfiction book, *Walk in My Combat Boots*. My partner was Sergeant Matt Eversmann. Matt's an interesting guy, definitely one of a kind. He's smart, modest, and courageous. Matt was the real-life sergeant portrayed in the movie *Black Hawk Down.*

Our partnership started like this: Matt and my friend Tim Malloy had done a documentary, *Send Me,* about medical advances in the military. They filmed it in Afghanistan. Matt did the on-camera interviews. I was struck by the way he got men and women talking about combat and their time in the military. That isn't easy.

When I'm interviewed on television, I frequently feel there's a screen between myself and the reporter. When Matt talked to military personnel in Afghanistan, there was no screen.

That gave me the idea for a book, and even the

title, *Walk in My Combat Boots*. I was certain that millions of Americans didn't really understand the military. Part of the reason is that many vets won't talk about their experiences. My father never told us about what he saw and did during World War II. Most of us have family members and friends who are tight-lipped or tongue-tied about their service.

But Matt Eversmann got his subjects for *Send Me* talking and baring their souls. He knew the right questions to ask and the right follow-up questions.

So we decided to work on *Walk in My Combat Boots* together. Matt did over a hundred interviews, forty- and fifty-pagers, which he, Chris Mooney, and I turned into tight, emotional five- to seven-page stories.

Admiral William McRaven, an eloquent writer himself, read *Walk in My Combat Boots* and gave us this humbling quote:

If you ever had a moment's doubt about the courage, the sense of duty, or the patriotism of this young generation, then this book will put that doubt to rest. Raw, authentic, and above all, inspiring, these are the stories America needs to hear about the remarkable young men and women who serve. If these challenging times caused you to lose hope, this book will reaffirm your faith in all that is good and honorable about this country.

I always hope every book will turn out great. Sometimes it doesn't happen that way. But it did with *Walk in My Combat Boots*. I love the book. So I wrote a letter and sent it to A. G. Sulzberger, chairman and publisher of the *New York Times*.

Dear Arthur,

I'm sending you Walk in My Combat Boots *in the hope that you will spend half an hour with it and read five or six of the servicemen and -women's true stories. I think you'll be surprised, and maybe understand my disappointment that the book was unable to get any coverage in the* New York Times. *I understand that an incredible number of books are published every week, but I know that readers come away from* Walk in My Combat Boots *understanding—often for the first time—what the military is all about. I also feel it's unusual that reading a book or watching a film can deliver this kind of impact. President Clinton told me he couldn't stop thinking about the stories in* Combat Boots *for several days. I was careful not to editorialize or bring any political agenda to the book. Rather, I simply edited and presented the stories and let them speak for themselves. I've said a few times now that* Walk in My Combat Boots *is the most important book I've written. Actually, it's probably the only important book I've done.*

All my best,
James Patterson

A few weeks later, I heard back from Arthur Sulzberger.

Mr. Patterson,

Thank you for taking the time to write, and for sending along a copy of your book. It was an unexpected surprise to hear from such an accomplished author. I'll look forward to reading the book, and I'm glad you've gotten such a positive response so far. As with all our journalism, I leave specific coverage decisions to our editors. But if you'd like me to put you in touch with Pamela Paul, who oversees the Review, *I'd be more than happy to. Either way, congratulations on the book and wishing you luck on your next project.*

Best wishes,
AG

I was glad that he took the time to write. I hope he also took the time to read *Walk in My Combat Boots*. I think it's important that people at the *New York Times* understand our military. That's hard for people—like me—who have never been shot at, who have never had to shoot at another human being, who have never put their lives on the line for others.

meet jimmy

MICHAEL PIETSCH, MY long-suffering editor, now the CEO of Little, Brown's parent company, Hachette, is a good guy. Really smart too. He's a devoted family man. He cares deeply about books. That's probably why—against all logic and common sense—he let me start my own kids' imprint, JIMMY Books, at Little, Brown.

This is how I finally sold Michael on the idea. I told him JIMMY's mission. Like all good business plans, it's deceptively simple, but I think it's spot-on:

"When a kid finishes a JIMMY book, he or she will say, 'Please give me another book.'"

Here's a sad alternative to that: *Millions of kids in this country have never read a single book that they love.* That's the truth.

So is the fact that tens of millions of our kids—over 50 percent of them across

America—*don't read at grade level.* That's so tragic, and avoidable, it's hard to fathom, hard to write about. And it's happening in the richest country in the world.

I know, I know, get off the soapbox.

In a minute.

Everywhere I go to speak, I hear the same thing from parents and grandparents: *I didn't know you write books for kids.* Well, now you know. What's more, I happen to believe my kids' books are the best books that I write. Just my opinion.

Here's what I have to offer your kids, or your grandkids, or the kids you teach in school.

I Funny. I wrote the book and the series with Chris Grabenstein. It tells the story of a precocious middle-school kid named Jamie Grimm. Jamie is aching to be a stand-up comedian. So he studies every comedian he can find. Real comedians, like Chris Rock, Groucho Marx, Jerry Seinfeld, Jim Gaffigan, Ellen DeGeneres, Wanda Sykes, John Mulaney. Then he starts writing his own stuff. He's funny. He wants to get funnier. A big twist in the story is that Jamie can never be a stand-up comedian. He's in a wheelchair.

Middle School: The Worst Years of My Life

was my first book for middle-school kids. Like *I Funny,* the Middle School books get kids smiling and reading more.

Pottymouth and Stoopid is even funnier. And it dares to take on the difficult subject of word-bullying. I'm obviously biased, but I highly recommend it.

Unfortunately, there seems to be an unwritten prejudice against books and movies that make kids laugh. Some adults in positions of authority think, *How serious can a book be if we're laughing at it?* Pretty damn serious. *Catch-22,* anyone? *Breakfast of Champions? A Confederacy of Dunces? Carry On, Jeeves? Diary of a Wimpy Kid?*

If they taught movies in school—and it wouldn't be such a terrible way to get kids thinking about structure and storytelling—but started with Ingmar Bergman movies, most of us would say, *Oh, I really don't like movies much.*

And that's what has happened with books in a lot of our schools. Way too often, kids are taught with Ingmar Bergman–style books. Millions and millions of kids are turned off to reading before they get a chance to fall in love with books.

It almost happened to me back in Newburgh

at St. Patrick's grammar school. The Domini-can nuns almost got me.

Parents come up to me all the time and say, "I can't get my kids reading." I commiserate, then I tell them, "Hey, do you manage to get them to the dinner table? Do you allow them to track mud or snow onto your living-room carpet? Do you let them curse in church?"

Then make this a rule: *We read in our house.*

what i blabber about to kids at elementary schools across the country

LISTEN! SHUSH! EYES to the front. Ears to the sides. There's one word I want you to memorize today. Just one word.

This one word will make school so much easier, and so much more fun.

Are you ready? Who's ready? I'm ready.

Outline, babies! Outline, outline, outline!

Outline your book reports, outline any speech you have to make in school, outline your e-mails, outline the texts you send to your friends.

I outlined this speech before I came to your school. *See how good it is?*

Also...

Please try to keep your brains open to new ideas.

You don't have to accept everything people tell you, but at least *listen* to what they have to say.

Keep those precious brains of yours open!

Open your beautiful, young brains and let the sunshine in!

Because if your mind is closed, then nothing new can get inside.

Let's think about that for a second. Closed mind—nothing gets inside.

Okay, now. In the spirit of open minds—try to walk in somebody else's shoes at least once a day. Maybe even twice a day.

What's it like for your poor teachers to have to put up with you rowdy, ill-tempered boys and girls? Just kidding. You're all very nice!

What's it like for the other kids in your class? I'm talking about every single kid in this school! What is school like for them? Please walk in their shoes.

Okay, and what's it like for your moms and dads? They think about you all the time. Especially your moms. Now it's time to think about them.

Another thing. This is kind of earth-shakingly important. If you're a bully—*stop it right now!*

Being a bully could mean you have stuff to work out at home. So try your best to work it out at home.

Now, I'm going to say this one more

time—whenever you have to write anything, especially anything longer than a post on Twitter—

What's the word? Let me hear it!

(*The kids all shout.*)

Yes. *Outline!* Excellent!

You all memorized it already.

Thank you, thank you, thank you. I love you.

Remember. Open your minds and let the sunshine in!

No more bullies as of today!

Outline!

Don't forget me. I'll never forget you! Someday I'll put you all in a book.

the secret to writing

suspense is—

—play with the reader's mind

THE DAY, AND it was a day, that writing started to be fun for me, the day things began to really click, was the day I stopped trying to write sentences and started writing stories.

Sentences are hard for me—as you can see—but stories flow naturally from my heart and head.

I have a unique writing style. For better or worse, maybe a little of both, I have a voice. Michael Connelly described my style like this: "What Jim does is boil a scene down to the single, telling detail, the element that defines a character or moves a plot along. It's what fires off the movie projector in the reader's mind."

I don't know how often I actually succeed at that, but it's what I try to do. And I think Mike Connelly is probably more perceptive about my writing than I am.

I'm pretty sure there are some good stories in this book, but I don't know if there are any really good sentences.

That sure wasn't one.

Elaine Petrocelli, the owner of one of the best bookstores in Marin County, California (or just about anywhere else), occasionally reads my books. She had a heart attack a while back. While Elaine was recovering in the hospital, she was given *1st to Die,* the first of my Women's Murder Club novels.

The idea for the Women's Murder Club came from an observation I had while working at J. Walter Thompson. It was my experience that many of the women at Thompson were more collaborative than the men. So I had an idea to put four women together in a mystery series—specifically, a detective, a medical examiner, a journalist, and an assistant district attorney. I wanted to see what would happen if they collaborated on the most difficult murder cases.

The other stimulus for the Women's Murder Club mystery series was my home life back in Newburgh. The tone of voice for the novels came out of real-life experiences with my mother and grandmother, my three incorrigible sisters, our female cat. Their *buzz* and *purr* are still inside my head. Like, *right now.* Drives me a little crazy!

In the first chapter of *1st to Die,* Lindsay Boxer, our detective, arrives at a San Francisco hotel. There's been a murder—*of course*—a beautiful couple on their beautiful honeymoon. *Have I no shame? No, none at all.* Next, we meet the medical examiner, Claire Washburn. She and Lindsay Boxer have worked on cases before. They're good friends. I'll stop right there—and get back to my favorite bookstore owner in Marin County.

Elaine Petrocelli told me, "A couple pages in, I had to put your damn book down! I'm in the hospital. I'm recovering from a heart attack. I cannot read a book called *1st to Die.* Tell me the ending."

I would not.

here's to the critics!

I LOVE THIS snarky line about critics. It comes from the English playwright John Osborne: "Asking a working writer how he feels about critics is like asking a lamp-post what it feels about dogs."

Actually, I'm all for critics. As long as they're honest. And they do their homework. A pretty smart critic at the *New York Times* once wrote that he hadn't finished any of my books but he knew he wouldn't like them. He came to this conclusion because a critic friend of his told him so. Sorry, but I don't buy that as either good criticism or good journalism.

When people bring up my practice of writing with coauthors, they usually aren't thinking nice thoughts. Here's the best defense I've come up with about cowriters.

Simon & Garfunkel
Lennon & McCartney

Lennon & McCartney & Harrison & Starr

Gilbert & Sullivan

Rodgers & Hammerstein

Woodward & Bernstein

Larry David & Jerry Seinfeld

Neil Gaiman & Terry Pratchett

Stephen King & Peter Straub

Douglas Preston & Lincoln Child

Joel & Ethan Coen

Matt Stone & Trey Parker

William Shakespeare & Christopher Marlowe & John Fletcher

I could go on. My point is that collaborations are common and they often work beautifully. They obviously succeed big-time in film and music, and for me they've been a good way to tell a lot of stories. And trust me, I have a lot of stories to tell.

While we're on the subject of cowriters, here's a line for somebody to use in a review of this book: "Surprisingly, Patterson's autobiography isn't half bad. I just wonder who wrote it for him."

That isn't true, but hell, put it up on the internet anyway. You know the operating principle—lies travel faster than the truth.

the great cowriting mystery, solved

I GUESS THE cowriting thing has to be talked about.

I have a few wonderful, crackerjack, masochistic cowriters whom I work with regularly. Every new book of mine starts with an outline. I write the outline—from fifty to eighty pages. The outline is specific about what each scene should be, and it's always about *scenes*. The outline lays out the core of the story, the plot, and often the tone of voice.

Next, I ask the cowriter to help. A lot. I do this for two selfish reasons. I want their smart thinking, but I also want them emotionally involved in the story. That's crucial for the book's success.

Generally, I ask for pages to be sent to me every two to three weeks. (This is the exact opposite of how it works at most publishing houses.) If the story is going the wrong way or is losing energy, I'll say things like "Hold on, let's talk this out. The story is starting to march in place." Or "I think we've lost track of what should be driving us ahead." Or "I'm losing interest in our narrator. That's probably the fault of my outline." Or "The story's voice is gone."

Then I make some very specific suggestions on how to improve things quickly, seamlessly, hopefully painlessly.

More often what I say is "Hooray. You're the best. Keep it up. I can't wait to read more pages." It seems to work fairly well.

I asked a few of the coconspirators—the ones smart enough to keep it civil—to share a few of their thoughts on whatever it is that we do together.

Peter de Jonge was my first collaborator and is a fine writer on his own. He's done several lengthy pieces in the *New York Times Magazine*. Impressive, right? You can see why Peter is my favorite cowriter.

One of the best things about working with Jim, and this may be the key to why he is a publishing juggernaut, is that he is almost pathologically open-minded. If an idea adds stakes or drama or weight or in any helpful way propels the story forward, he's game. As he told me once, you can tell any story you want, but it has to be a story.

David Ellis and I have worked together on several books, including *The Black Book*—which is probably my favorite thriller. The main character, Billy Harney, is right up there with Alex Cross. David wrote this about our experience working together. (He was just trying to butter me up.) By the way, Dave is my favorite cowriter.

I always felt like Jim was doing more than collaborating with me. He was trying to teach me. And it was always about respecting the reader. The only question is, how will the reader respond? If it heightens the drama for the reader—because it makes you love the protagonist or hate the villain...because it tears at your heart; because it turns your expectations upside down—then it belongs in the book.

Jim Born used to do research for Elmore Leonard. He's an ex-DEA agent out of Miami. If there's such a thing as a quiet wild man, that's Born. No wonder Jim is my favorite cowriter.

After a career in police work, followed by the solitary life of a writer, I didn't know what to expect when I started working with Jim. The most important way it changed my approach to writing is in Jim's use of an outline. I had never written from an outline before. Now, eleven books later, I will never write another book without an outline. Jim reminds me of some of my bosses in police work: To the point, efficient, blunt, and empowering. And funny. He can lay down burns as well as any cop I've ever met.

Mark Sullivan went to Hamilton College in upstate New York, just like my dad and my pal Tim Malloy. All that terrific education and Mark ends up writing suspense novels, like his huge bestseller *Beneath a Scarlet Sky*. No wonder Mark is my favorite cowriter.

Jim is always in favor of changes if the changes make the tale more terrific. He also forced me to constantly be aware of our characters and their private lives and the dramatic forces and emotional stakes in every scene. Jim can be withering in his criticism and effusive in his praise. He's generous to a fault and you can't get better understanding or advice about the publishing business. Most of all, Jim's made me a better storyteller and writer. What could be better than that?

Maxine Paetro keeps the Women's Murder Club on a very tight leash. She's so damn *logical*. And smart. We are huge telephone pals and I adore her. And of course, Max is my favorite cowriter.

I was snug on my couch, my head in San Francisco as I steamed toward the finish line of the new Women's Murder Club thriller I was writing with Jim. The phone rang. It was Jim.

"Max. I have a book for us. It's called *Woman of God.*"

Jim told me about his character, Brigid

Fitzgerald, a young Catholic doctor who takes a job in a displaced-persons settlement in South Sudan. Brigid is twenty-six years old and will become one of six doctors in a community of 80,000 people barely surviving in dire conditions.

Jim had an idea that in the future, Brigid might become pope. *A woman pope.* It was a huge idea, but for me?

I said, "Jim, I can't help you write this one. I'm not Catholic. I'm not even a Christian."

He said, "Every time you think *Catholic woman,* think *strong woman.* You're a strong woman, Max. Write that. This will be your favorite book."

I was doubtful. But after reading and rereading Jim's deeply plotted outline, I researched the Church and the poverty, disease, and massacres in South Sudan. I thought, *Maybe I can do this.*

In the end, Jim was right. (He's irritating that way.) *Woman of God* is my favorite book.

Brendan DuBois was hiding out in New Hampshire (I suspect he's part of the Witness Protection Program) when I read a couple of his award-winning short stories. I gave him a phone call. He made the mistake of answering. And now he's my favorite cowriter.

One quickly learns Jim's terms. "These pages are great" is the highest praise one can receive. But "I'm just not buying it" means back to the keyboard. But Jim is a true collaborator, rarely telling you how to fix something, usually leaving it up to you to figure it out.

Richard DiLallo was one of my fellow Mad Men who discovered there was life after advertising. I've also worked with his brilliant wife, Susan, and one of his sons, Max. Richard and Susan are keeping their triplets away from me. With so much in common, Richard is my favorite cowriter.

A really good thing about writing with Jim is that you feel he believes in you. He thinks you're good. That kind of respect is very empowering. You're free to be inventive, creative, surprising. He may not always agree with you, but you do feel that he was happy you went on the journey.

Chris Grabenstein is one of the funniest people I know. He's also a total sweetheart in every way. No wonder Chris is my favorite cowriter.

I was lucky enough to first meet Jim back when I was a junior copywriter and he was the executive creative director at J. Walter Thompson. I can still remember our very first "writing lesson." I was in the ad agency's Professional Development Program. Jim was giving a lunchtime lecture to all us trainees in a very posh Madison Avenue conference room.

Back in those days, Jim had a very bushy beard.

Anyway, he stood behind the lectern at the front of the conference room as we trainees sat eagerly in our seats ready to take notes and learn from the master.

"This afternoon, I will teach you how to make a million dollars a year writing advertising," he started. "The secret is—"

Before he could say another word, some knucklehead came charging into the conference room with a banana cream pie and *slammed* it into Jim's face. Whipped cream and graham cracker crumb crust and oozing yellow pie filling dribbled down and clung to his beard. The pie-thrower was long gone but I know what all the trainees in that room were thinking: *That guy is so fired! He pied James Patterson!*

Jim cleaned himself up a little, wiped away the whipped cream, clasped the sides of the lectern, and said, "Okay. I just showed you how to make a million dollars a year writing advertising. Throw a pie in their face and, once you have their attention, say something smart."

That was my first lesson from Jim and one I never forgot. It's also why everything we write together starts with a *bang* and lots of action. We're still throwing pies in our readers' faces.

Of course, I have other coconspirators, but I don't completely trust them to say really, really nice things about me. But even though I don't trust them, each and every one is my favorite cowriter.

nobody moves,
nobody gets hurt

the movieholic

MY TASTE IN movies is maddeningly, almost irrationally eclectic. I try not to talk about what's best, just my personal favorites. Here's one example. Back in 2015, my top two couldn't have been more different—*Carol* and *Mad Max: Fury Road*. One of my all-time favorites is *Godfather II*. I thought *Pulp Fiction* was a one-of-a-kind film, and that goes for most of Quentin Tarantino's movies. I didn't like *Chinatown* that much the first time I saw it, but when I watched it a second time, I changed my mind—you know, *flip-flopped*. I was stunned by how artfully composed every scene was. I felt the same way about Alfonso Cuarón's *Roma*.

I was blown away in the theater watching *The Silence of the Lambs,* but not for the reasons you might expect. At the film's end, we have Dr. Frederick Chilton casually walking away from the camera. You'll probably remember that Chilton ran the prison where convicted serial killer Hannibal Lecter was housed. Chilton hadn't done anything particularly evil. He did leer at Clarice Starling, and he was unpleasant to Lecter, *the serial killer*. But at the end of the movie, the audience gets the sense that Lecter is going to chase Chilton down, kill him, possibly eat him. And they cheer! I kind of get it—but that's really, really crazy. And that's probably why I'm addicted to movies.

I will never forget taking Jeanne Galleta, my girlfriend in high school, to see *Psycho*. Neither Jeanne nor I could sleep or shower for weeks after watching Hitchcock's creepy masterpiece. The *Psycho* remake of 1998 had one of the funnier taglines ever: "The classic story of a boy and his mother."

Sue and I just watched *Something's Gotta Give* again. Diane Keaton is perfect in every scene, almost in every take. Where was her Academy Award? C'mon, Academy members, it's time for a recount.

Sometimes I run into fans of mine in movie theaters (at least I used to, before COVID). A lot of people who read my books seem to go to the movies. They'll come up and tell me that I got their kids or their grandkids reading. Many of them tear up—probably because it's so scary when your kid is having trouble in school. There's no better compliment I can get than "You got my kids reading."

A few years back, PBS ran a vote-for-your-favorite-novel contest. Eventually, they announced the winner—*To Kill a Mockingbird.* What a shocker that was. Personally, I liked *Mockingbird,* but not as much as some people.

Anyway, Jimmy Kimmel covered the contest on his show. He announced, "Nobody reads novels anymore." Then he proceeded to interview six or seven nitwits in LA. Each of them said something like "I've never read a novel. I don't read novels."

I know Kimmel was trying to be funny. He *is* funny. Maybe he was taking a sly poke at the PBS crowd or a few sunstruck idiots in LA, but when I watched the show, my response was "Screw you, Jimmy!"

I'm sure fewer people *read* novels than *don't* these days, but making reading seem uncool—is, well, uncool. It's also a tragedy for this oft-times wrongheaded country of ours. Especially when it affects kids, which it obviously does.

here's a tip for other writers

WHAT'S THE SINGLE most valuable thing I've learned in publishing? If you put a product you really like in your book, chances are pretty good the company that makes it will send you free stuff. Maybe even a case of stuff. Watch and learn.

Favorite wine: A tie—Caymus Special Selection and Pahlmeyer

Favorite chocolates: Another tie—Godiva and M&M's with peanuts

Favorite ice cream: Graeter's, especially strawberry chocolate chip or just plain chocolate chocolate chip

Favorite golf balls: Titleist Pro V

Golf-club memberships: Augusta National (How about a free round?)

Favorite camera: Leica

Favorite car: Tesla S

Favorite jet: Gulfstream 650

Favorite cookie: The fat Oreos with lots of cream in the center

By the way, this little chapter is an inside-baseball joke. It's just for the writers. But you know what, I bet I get some free Double Stuf Oreos out of it.

jock stories

THE BIG HOTSHOT jock in our house, no contest, is my wife, Sue. And she knows it. Sue was a high-school All-American, a four-time All-American swimmer at the University of Wisconsin–Madison, and a Big 10 champion and record holder.

Sue still swims every day, and I mean every day—in all kinds of weather. I've watched her swim while snow is falling.

Just keep swimming. Just keep swimming. Just keep swimming. Hey, it worked for Nemo.

I always felt that our job with our son, Jack, was to open doors for him—not to shove him through those doors, but just keep opening them. One door that he wouldn't let us open very wide was athletics. He's a good tennis player, a good skier, but for some reason, he doesn't believe that he's good. *Jack—you're good!*

I was a decent high-school baseball player, a better-than-decent high-school basketball player, an above-average golfer. I guess I was always a frustrated jock, but I'm over it now.

I'm sort of over it.

Recently I threw out a first pitch at a Yankees game. Sixty-some-thousand fans. I got it to home plate, but the pitch was a total piece of crap. I took some heat from my oldest friends, and they are *old*.

So, fine—I'm not completely over sports.

Sue is totally sick of hearing this next sports story. It took place a few years back. At that time, Sue had four holes in one in golf; I had three.

On February 6 of that year, I had another hole in one. Sue, who is nice in most ways but who's very competitive, said, "I don't like it, but I can live with it."

Two days later, on February 8, Sue and I went golfing together. I had another hole in one. Two in three days. That's insane. Almost unheard of. Ask anybody who golfs. Ask somebody at *Golf* magazine or *Sports Illustrated*. Ask Tiger Woods. I'll bet he's never done it.

Anyway, Sue and I are standing on the tee box and we watch the little white ball disappear into the relatively small hole that's a hundred and sixty-three yards away. Does she give me a big hug? *No*. Does she say, "Nice shot, honey"? *No way*.

She looks at me and very appropriately says, "You've got to be shitting me."

And that's the last thing I'll say about sports. Oh—did I mention I could dunk a basketball in high school? I think I did. Stephen King could never dunk. Neither could Dan Brown. Or Mailer, or Baldwin.

Just one more sports story.

A couple of my old friends kept playing basketball well into their fifties. They were in a men's league with mostly younger guys. My friends weren't all that good anymore, but they had the best team T-shirts in the league. The shirts said NOBODY MOVES, NOBODY GETS HURT.

And that's it for sports.

that catholic-school training really sticks with you

AS YOU KNOW by now, I was raised Roman Catholic, and raised hard. Kind of like Pinkie in Graham Greene's *Brighton Rock,* except that I didn't become a killer. I just write about them. My mother taught for peanuts and wooden nickels at St. Patrick's parish school. There were priests, nuns, and brothers in our house all the time.

Not once but twice, a Christian Brother borrowed one of our cars and crashed it into a tree.

These days—the days since COVID arrived—I don't know exactly what to make of God. I don't know if He or She or They know what to make of me, of us, and whatever it is we're collectively doing to destroy the Earth.

I personally don't think we can have intimate conversations with God.

I don't believe or understand why we should

expect a prayer to help our favorite football or basketball team win its next game. (Sue prays for the Wisconsin Badgers, but that's her problem. And actually, it seems to work a lot. Except when they play Ohio State in football.) Anyway, I also don't believe that God wants to hear from me on a regular basis. Of course, if God does want to know my story, God can just read this book.

No offense meant.

Hopefully, none taken.

love stories

hugs

HUGS ARE IMPORTANT in life. I think they should count for a lot more than money in the bank.

My father was a very private person, especially around our house. I don't blame him, but I never felt that I knew who he was. He kept *himself* bottled up inside. I probably do some of that too.

A telling moment came during a "celebration" of my father's life. My sister Carole orchestrated it a few months after he died. She invited several of his friends, including people who had worked closely with him at Prudential headquarters in Boston.

His friends and coworkers sat around and told the most charming, funny, quite lovely stories about my father, whom they all called Pat.

At one point, Carole and I turned to one

another and she whispered, "Jimmy, *who* are they talking about?" Carole and I had never seen this side of my father, the one they all called Pat. We wondered whether my mother had ever met Pat.

I don't remember a single time I got a hug from my dad. Not as a little kid, or a teenager, or a grown-up. Not until he was on his deathbed.

My father had been a drinker and a heavy smoker into his sixties. Not surprisingly, he developed heart problems. When Dad was in his late seventies, I got a call from Carole that he had been hospitalized up in Massachusetts.

I jumped on a plane and was in my father's hospital room that afternoon.

We talked and talked, and we finally hugged.

I never forgot that moment, the feel of holding him in my arms, his diminished shape pressed against my chest. My father even told me that he loved me. That was another first for us. I told Dad that I loved him. *Charles and James.* After all those years, we finally came together.

Less than a week later, he was gone.

Here's what I took away from those last few days, the lesson I learned and took to heart.

From the time Jack was a little kid until now, every single night before he goes to bed, I go into his room and give him a big hug.

I tell Jack that I love him, and he tells me that he loves me back.

nan and pop

IF YOU WANT to blame one person, and that seems to be the way of the world these days, my grandmother on my mother's side made me what I am today. Nan only got through eighth grade. Pop left school after sixth grade. They married at sixteen. Both were bright, always fair, always fun to be around. But I never saw either one of them crack open a book. Still, they pushed me to be my best and not squander my gifts, if I had any gifts to squander.

My grandparents were definitely hard workers. Over the years, Nan and Pop ran two candy stores and two ice cream stores, and they owned a small restaurant and bar called Fieldstone Lodge. They built the lodge themselves, literally built it. Then they built a house on the hill behind the restaurant. Who do you know today who can build their own house?

Pop used to tell me that my right to extend my arm ended at the next person's nose. He and Nan weren't biased against anybody.

When I was in grade school, they rented out a small cottage they'd built behind the main house to two women from nearby Stewart Air Force Base. One morning, Nan ushered my sister Mary Ellen and me into her cozy breakfast nook. She made cocoa, sliced some warm babka, then told us that we might hear some stories about the air force women, Betty and Lou, but we should ignore all the small-minded talk. Betty and Lou were good people. They loved each other. And they were our dear friends. That attitude toward gay women wasn't exactly the norm back in the 1950s. But it was the norm for Nan and so it became the norm for our family. I'm not trying to be self-righteous here, just telling the story like it happened.

Pop was a totally lovable guy too. When he ran the Fieldstone Lodge, a DUI wasn't as big a deal as it is now. Actually, I think it was called a DWI back then. If a customer of his tried to drive home under the influence, Pop would ask for his keys and drive him home himself. He'd say, "You know where your car is, my friend. It's safe and sound right here in the lot of the Fieldstone Lodge, and it'll be here safe and sound in the morning."

Nan and Pop. I loved them both. Still do.

those blue fortune cookies

JOHN KERESTY WAS my best friend for over twenty years, much too short a run on the planet, in my opinion. John had been one of the youngest newspaper editors in chief in the country at the *Ridgewood News*. He chose to write most of the paper's sports news, because he liked sports, and, man, he absolutely *loved* to go to the racetrack.

Keresty had a system for betting horses that was genius, at least if you wanted to have some fun at the track. Let's face it, though: people aren't there to have fun — they are at the race-track to suffer and lose.

Here's the Keresty method. He'd look at the tout sheet for each race, then figure out which horse had the biggest discrepancy between the tout-sheet odds and the current odds at the track. His theory was that in all but the highest-stakes races, most of the better horses were pretty much equal. So he would bet the decent horse with the best odds. And he'd bet win, place, and show. That meant that much of the time, he'd get to go to the window and collect some money instead of tearing up the betting slips in disgust. Even if you lost a little, you'd make it up in fun. I don't go to the track often, but when I do, I use the Keresty method.

A couple of years ago, our friends Jim and Irene Karp named one of their horses Patterson Cross. PC turned into the most beautiful grown-up horse, and against all odds, he won races at Gulfstream and Sarasota.

I had to go against the Keresty method to bet on Patterson Cross because he sometimes went off as a favorite or close to it. He was trained by Kentucky Derby winner Bill Mott at Claiborne Farm in Paris, Kentucky. When Sue and I visited Claiborne Farm with the Karps, we were shown a graveyard there for famous racehorses. I guess the Karps thought any mystery writer worth his salt would want to visit a horse graveyard.

As it turns out, they only bury the horse's

head (intelligence), heart (courage), and hooves (speed). With one exception. When they interred Secretariat in 1989, they buried the entire horse. That little nugget of horse history was definitely worth the trip to Paris.

Kentucky.

Getting back to my friend Johnny Keresty: He didn't have much of a singing voice, but he loved music. Every year around Christmas, he'd invite several of us to the Brandenburg Concertos performed by the Chamber Music Society of Lincoln Center. Before the show, John would treat the group to a big meal at the four-star restaurant Shun Lee West.

At the end of the feast, the restaurant always serves fortune cookies. One night we opened the cookies and none of us could believe what we saw. The paper messages went something like *You will get a blow job tonight* and *You will stroke a beautiful penis*. Now, you have to understand, Shun Lee is a pretty fancy New York restaurant—but Keresty had found a way to get them to deliver "blue" fortune cookies to his table. That was my friend, and I have lots of Johnny Keresty stories.

I only wish I had more.

———

Here's the best I've come up with about recovering from the death of somebody we love. It goes like this.

When we're little, maybe one or so, we learn how to walk. Somehow we figure out how to get up on our two feet and take a scary step forward.

Maybe we fall down. But we get up again. We take another step.

We move forward. We move on.

We just don't forget.

gone but not forgotten

I TREASURE THE time I spend with close friends and I've come to understand lately that you never know which visit could be the last. A friend of mine, Joe Denyeau, who, like Keresty, died way too young, used to tell a story about the bitter end of his Wall Street career. Joe had worked there from his early twenties into his late thirties.

One of his brothers had been ill with terminal cancer, and Joe spent a lot of time with him during the last days of the illness. All the while, he was working sixty hours a week on Wall Street.

At his brother's funeral, Joe got an *urgent* call from his Wall Street office. His boss demanded that he return to work immediately. I know there's a tough-guy, take-no-prisoners culture at a lot of successful companies. I get it. But to me, that isn't culture. It's boorish greed, and I hate it with a passion that burns deep.

Instead of returning to his job, Joe went back into the church. He sat down with his wife and family. After the service, he told his wife, Anne, about the phone call. Then he told her something else—his Wall Street career was over. True to his word, and himself, Joe quit his job at Lehman Brothers the next day.

Not too long ago, Sue and I attended the funeral of our friend Steve Bowen. Steve's two sons gave emotional but also funny eulogies. Their words were totally appropriate. Steve would've approved, even applauded his boys' good work, their storytelling.

Then the parish priest got up and talked about Steve. This priest had been married at one time. When his wife died, he'd joined the priesthood. (Yes, it's allowed.) The priest's eulogy wasn't one of those deflating messes cobbled together with mismatched platitudes and Bible quotes. This priest knew his subject well. And he told a classic Bowen story.

He said that near the end for Steve, he had gone to visit him at Dana-Farber in Boston. The priest got to the door of Steve's room. And he stopped dead in his tracks. Steve was staring at him from his hospital bed. Now, Catholics are really into the afterlife and heaven. That's important to the story. Steve kept staring at the priest, pointed a rigid finger at him, and said in a voice that was still stentorian, "You'd better be right."

God bless Steve Bowen. And I definitely hope the parish priest was right.

mj

MJ, MARY JORDAN, probably isn't expecting this, but if she is, she'd never let me know. She's been my right hand and my left, my loyal, trusted personal assistant since we began working together at J. Walter Thompson in 1996.

She has my back. She protects me from everybody, friends and enemies alike. She gets raves from strangers she's had to deal with on the phone or through e-mails and texts.

She's typing this damn book for me. She'll probably edit and rewrite this chapter. Or maybe she'll just throw it the hell out. She puts up with me when I'm ornery or short-tempered, tries to laugh at my bad jokes, counsels me when I'm doing something half-assed.

She went with me to transcribe the first Q&A between myself and President Clinton.

He grinned at her. "So you're the famous Mary Jordan!"

Occasionally, MJ is misunderstood by people who think she's too protective—but more often than not, it's people who want to keep her in her place and who don't understand that she doesn't have a place. She's MJ. She's her own person, beholden to no one. Not even me.

She's yet another Catholic. MJ's mom kept up the garden and flowers in her parish in Carmel, New York. When she died, she was so beloved at the church that two priests, two monsignors, and a deacon conducted the service together. I guarantee that Pope Francis won't get a better funeral Mass.

Mary loved her mom and the service couldn't have been more beautiful.

mystery lady

ONE MYSTERY I never solved has to do with a friend I had during junior and senior years in college. We dated and sent letters back and forth for a year and a half.

For some reason, I could never be myself around her. I think she scared me a little. Who can tell about things of the heart, especially young, inexperienced hearts.

I remember late one night, we were in Van Cortlandt Park walking under a full moon and about a hundred billion stars. I thought it was kind of beautiful, kind of poetic. She was beautiful and kind of poetic herself. She looked at me and seemed confused. "Jim, what are we doing out here?"

Good question. Fair question. She was probably right, but from that night on, the disconnect between us grew wider. After a party at Ned Mahoney and B. J. Stringer's, we slept together. Nothing happened, which was okay. The two of us figured out that this—whatever it was—wasn't going anywhere special. It was a little heartbreaking at the time. No one's fault. Just life doing its life thing.

In our forties, the Mystery Lady and I reconnected and went for a drink or two at the Algonquin Hotel in Manhattan. We told a couple of war stories, enjoyed the fact that we had nice careers that we loved. But after all the years, something was still a little off. She married, and recently I heard her husband died. Another writer. I wish her all the best.

Not really a love story, I guess. More an unrequited-puppy-love story, at least for me. They build character, and I'm still working on my character.

still dating—after all these years

AFTER JANE DIED, suddenly I was "available," which meant, ready or not, I was eligible to date again, to get back into the pool, to enter the New York meat market. I hadn't liked dating rituals when I was in my twenties. A decade later, I was scared to death of them.

I soon found out that dating in New York was more complicated than ever, and maybe even more desperate. Meeting somebody in a bar had never made a lot of sense to me—not unless your dream person was potentially an alcoholic. I liked the movie *You've Got Mail,* but I didn't honestly believe I would find true love in a bookstore.

So, of course, I did something worse. This was *so* dumb.

I walked into the East Side offices of a dating service called It's Just Lunch. I don't know why but this move seemed completely rational to me, or at least harmless.

Wrong, wrong, wrong.

As I entered the office, I was thinking, *This isn't desperate. I'm not pathetic. This isn't creepy. It's just lunch.*

A woman who said she was a partner gave me a longish questionnaire to fill out. I was supposed to complete it right there in the office. So I started in and was trying to be as honest as I could possibly be. And hopeful. Positive.

But I found I didn't have answers for some of the rather vaguely worded questions.

So I sheepishly approached the executive who had given me the questionnaire. I told her my problem—*my* problem, not a problem with their questionnaire.

I think I was being nice. I just wanted to be honest about answering the questions.

But the partner got angry with me. And, yes, this really happened. She told me to leave. "Right now. You can go."

I walked back out on the street, which was crowded, lots of honking horns, city buses doing their bus-exhaust thing, and I couldn't believe what had just happened.

I'd just been shot down—*by a dating service.*

people who need people

PEOPLE **MAGAZINE CALLED** soon after the dating-service disaster, and as it turned out, they wanted to talk about my love life.

Seriously? What love life?

This was supposed to be an interview about my rising career as a mystery novelist, but the reporter knew I had recently lost someone. I told her I didn't want to talk about Jane. It was too soon. Too personal. My feelings were too raw. The reporter for *People* insisted. So I told her as little as possible and moved on to the much safer topic of Alex Cross's latest multiple-murder case.

A month or so later, the piece ran in *People*. It was about this pleasant-enough writer guy in his thirties, living by himself in a beautiful apartment overlooking Central Park, where he was in mourning for the woman he loved.

The week after the article appeared in *People* magazine, I got over fifteen hundred letters and packages from as far away as Germany. The letters, the poetry, the photographs came from women of all ages and also quite a few men. I was invited to dinner, to lunch (take that, It's Just Lunch), to have coffee, to write back, to call on the phone, to come visit in Buffalo, Terre Haute, San Juan, Berlin. Almost all of the letters were sympathetic, human, sometimes funny, occasionally sad. I actually responded to two of them, but in the end, I remained in the deep end of the dating pool.

Why did I keep going? I think it was because I knew from my experience with Jane how good a relationship could be. I had hope. I wasn't cynical. I wasn't afraid. No matter what happened next, I wasn't going to give up.

Finally, I asked Sue Solie out—which was where I should've started in the first place.

Right at the top.

Actually, it was my work friend Frank Nicolo who inadvertently served as a matchmaker for Sue and me. As Frank put it himself:

I believe this happened in the fall of 1996. After Jim and I finished work we had dinner together. On this momentous night, we were eating at a Cajun restaurant on the Upper East Side. The place is long gone. As fate would have it, Sue Solie walked by the restaurant. Sue waved. Jim and I waved back, and Sue went on her way. Allow me to drift back to the early 1980s. Sue, a very beautiful and very talented young woman, came to work with us at J. Walter Thompson as an art director. There's no doubt she caught the eye of every guy in the place. By 1996, Jim and I had been working with Sue for about a dozen years. Now fast-forward to that fateful night. At that time Sue was newly divorced. After Sue passed by, I looked at Jim and said, "You're single. Sue's single. Why not ask her out?" "You really think so?" he responded. "Yeah," I said, "give it a shot." So he did, and less than a year later they married. Funny how a moment can change lives. Sue waved. Jim waved. And that was that.

my best friend, my girl, my sweetheart of sweethearts

YOU'VE ALREADY HEARD a lot about Sue, but not the best parts, not the juicy stuff, not the heart of the heart of the love story.

Susan Solie Patterson and I have been great friends for over thirty years. We were married in 1997, and we're *still* best friends. Actually, it's so much more than that. I adore her. It's never been an issue of whether she can keep up with me; it's whether I can keep up with Sue.

I can't.

One of our secrets is that we consider ourselves incredibly lucky to have found one another. We don't want to do anything to mess that up. Another key is that we spend most days together but we give each other lots of room to do other things. No jealousy allowed. No changing ourselves to be what the other person wants or expects. That's always a bad idea, in my opinion.

While I was busy shimmying up the ladder at J. Walter Thompson, Sue married another writer who worked there. She left the agency soon after that. Sue returned to Thompson years later and she was single again. I saw her from time to time in the halls. Her smile remained dazzling, she hadn't lost her sense of humor or her wit, and she looked pretty good too.

I finally asked her out to dinner, and Sue told me not to pick her up, she would meet me at a restaurant on the West Side. (She's always been the boss of us.) I was excited about our first date, but I was nervous. Sue and I had been dancing around this moment, this *date,* for a lot of years. I'd hated it when she married that other writer.

So I got to the restaurant early. Half an hour later, then forty-five minutes later, Sue hadn't shown up.

I was friends with the maître d', and she sat down with me, assured me that whoever my no-show date was, she wasn't worth the long face. My dinner for one would be on the house. I had to pay for my wine, though. I was already on my second glass.

Then Sue showed up—windblown, perspiring, apologizing nonstop.

She hadn't been able to flag down a cab during rush hour, and she'd run all the way from her apartment on the East Side. Her smile was still dazzling, and I thought she looked pretty damn good, even windblown and perspiring and slightly off her game.

We talked about a trip she'd just made home to Illinois, the movies *Shine* and *Fargo,* the best sneakers out there, my most recent Alex Cross novel, the latest J. Walter gossip, the insanity of dating in New York City.

We kept jabbering until the restaurant closed and my maître d' friend finally had to shoo us out. She even gave me a little pat on the butt.

Sue told me that she'd never talked with anybody like that before—especially not her ex. We kissed outside the restaurant. First kiss. Sweet kiss. Kind of dizzying. I'll leave it at that—because that's all that happened.

Five months later, I picked Sue up for another dinner date. We were going to Windows on the World in the World Trade Center.

First, though, we had to make an unscheduled stop at St. Patrick's Cathedral. I had always loved the neo-Gothic cathedral and so did Sue, who was kind of Catholic and kind of Lutheran. Long story for another book.

We walked all the way down the center aisle to the very first row. Man, I still loved the smell of incense. I got down on one knee and tried something I'd never done before. I proposed.

I don't know this for sure, but I think I was appropriately eloquent, and definitely emotional and sincere. I was madly in love.

Sue looked into my eyes—we both have very blue eyes—and I remember exactly what she said: *"Sure."* Then she punctuated "Sure" with that irresistible smile of hers.

To be honest, every once in a while, there's an hour or two when I can't stand Sue—but there isn't a day that goes by that I'm not in love with her.

She had me at "Sure" and she still does. Here's the thing: If Sue ever leaves me, I'm going with her.

sue speaks for herself

I MET JIM in 1983 when I was looking for a job in advertising. I'd recently graduated from the University of Wisconsin–Madison with an MFA and I wanted to be an art director. This was back in the day when we didn't have e-mails, and handwritten letters were the way to go. Most ad agencies sent back form letters—but J. Walter Thompson wrote back a note with a direct phone number. I started to keep in touch with the creative department's head of personnel, Garland Goode. My mother, for some reason, was adamant about my getting an interview at Thompson. *She must've known.*

After months of persistence, I got Garland Goode to look at my portfolio. She showed it to Jim while I was waiting out in the lobby.

Ten minutes later she poked her head out the door and said, "Mr. Patterson has been looking for someone like you for a long time." (Little did he know, ha-ha.) My mom got some skin in the game too. Garland called her and said I shouldn't take the job I'd been offered at Ogilvy and Mather because "Mr. Patterson wants to hire her."

It only took thirteen years for him to ask me out on a date.

The day Jim and I were married was probably the worst (weather) day of the summer of 1997. It stopped pouring just long enough for us to say "I do" on the seventeenth green at Sleepy Hollow Country Club. We chose it because Jim had written a novel called *Miracle on the 17th Green*. It had seemed like a cool idea, and, except for the weather, it was.

We had invited his sisters and my two best friends as our witnesses, along with another friend, a judge, who wore a black robe and golf shoes (nice touch). The ceremony was intimate and very special. Jim held an umbrella over our heads the entire time. I don't think I felt a drop of rain.

He was so thoughtful about making our wedding day memorable. He traipsed around New York City looking at hotel after hotel to find just the right room for our wedding night. As I knew he would, he found a spectacular one, on Central Park South. It had the most stunning view of the park.

The day before the wedding, he went by the hotel just to make sure everything was perfect. It wasn't. Actually, it was a disaster. Turns out the sultan of Brunei was staying in the room and he wouldn't leave (he was an owner of the hotel). So we got the next best room in the place and a lot of gifts for our inconvenience.

Jim gave me a present every day of our honeymoon on the islands of Maui and Lanai in Hawaii. So sweet and thoughtful and, of course, creative. I still have them all.

One more quick memory. I'll never forget a very special day in the summer of 1997. Jim had rushed out to the drugstore to buy an early pregnancy test. While I was busy in the bathroom, I could hear him popping a bottle of champagne even before he knew the results.

Jim was right. Jack was in the house.

sweet lorraine

SUE WROTE A novel with a friend of ours, Susan DiLallo. It was inspired by the Susans' close relationship—sometimes *too close*—with their mothers, both of whom died the year they started their book. It's a doozy of a novel. Great pace. Heartfelt. Mother-daughter relationships deserve nothing less. The novel also has a terrific title: *Things I Wish I Told My Mother*. It will be published in the spring of 2023. Don't miss it.

I loved Sue's mom, my mother-in-law, as much as I loved my own mother.

Lorraine grew up out in the sticks but she still found her way into the class of 1943 at Wisconsin–Madison. She wanted to major in economics but in those days that was frowned upon for a woman. So she had a double major—economics and nursing. She probably could have run J. P. Morgan or Barclays one day, but instead she ran the emergency room at

UW Hospital. Until she had her one and only baby, Susan Lori.

Lorraine and her husband, OB, were the ultimate Badgers (they met at Wisconsin–Madison). For over fifty years, they attended almost every football game, plus at least half the basketball and hockey games.

Here's a story that's pure Lorraine and captures her great spirit. At ninety-eight, she won the family's college football pool. That's no mean feat, since the whole extended family—especially Sue's favorite cousin (this makes no sense to me), Mark Ormson—are irrationally out-of-control football maniacs. Lorraine's prize for winning the pool was a football signed by Wisconsin's athletic director, Barry Alvarez. Sue wanted to take Lorraine's picture and send it to Barry, who is a family friend. Lorraine balked, then *insisted* on getting her hair done first.

Then she did a perfect "Heisman pose," holding the prize football under one arm, the other arm extended to ward off tacklers. Barry Alvarez wrote back: "Lorraine, your hair looks great. And way to tote the rock."

Sweet Lorraine. She finally passed away close to her ninety-ninth birthday. As they used to say back in her day, *What a gal.*

the other love of my life

SUE IS A patient, indefatigable, loving mom who deserves the credit for raising our son, Jack, to be the man that he is. I remember Jack's first few minutes at Lenox Hill Hospital. I'd read or heard somewhere that newborns can't really discern much more than shapes, but as the delivery nurse held him, Jack cocked his head and checked me out for a few seconds.

Then he looked at Sue for a full minute. Makes sense. Sue is much better-looking than me, even right after giving birth.

Jack has always been a good storyteller, though he says he has zero interest in being a writer. I can't blame him for that. The kid is smart. "Phi Beta Jacka" at Brown, as we joke and try to keep his head from swelling.

When he was five, I had to go out to

Hollywood on business. I asked Jack, "Are you going to miss me?"

Our little five-year-old shook his head back and forth. "No, not really," he said.

That threw me for a loop, startled me, for sure. "You're not going to miss me?"

Jack shook his head again and said, "Not really, Daddy." Then he dropped the punch line on me. "Love means you can never be apart."

And he says he doesn't want to be a writer. Hell, he's probably secretly writing a novel and already has a book deal.

When Jack was a little older, I told him that any good lines that he came up with while living in our house belonged to me. So here I am using one: *Love means you can never be apart.*

At six or seven, Jack wrote and illustrated his first novel, *Death of the Butterfly Catcher.*

It opens with the Butterfly Catcher boarding a plane. He travels halfway around the world. Doesn't catch the butterfly. Next, the Butterfly Catcher gets on a boat. Travels another great distance. Doesn't catch the butterfly. Finally, he gets on a train. Jack *loved* trains as a kid. The Butterfly Catcher catches the butterfly on the train. He gets off. Isn't looking. Gets hit by a train going the other way. *Death of the Butterfly Catcher*. The butterfly flies away.

Jack has the gift. Good beginning, middle, and end. A perfect story.

From the perfect son.

prep school

PALM BEACH, WHERE we live most of the year, is about a million miles away from Newburgh, New York. My gentle, mostly respectful joke about Palm Beach is that it's a town of used-to-bes: used-to-be president of, used-to-be CEO of, used-to-be spouse of the used-to-be president or CEO.

We brought Jack up here and it was pretty idyllic for the three of us. Jack's school friends were low-key and down-to-earth in spite of their parents' wealth and, in some cases, fame.

The first bump in the road came when it was time for Jack to go to high school. Or, as it turned out, time to go to prep school. The concept of prep school had never entered my head as a kid growing up in upstate New York. Why would it? In those days nobody from Newburgh went to prep school. The same was true for Sue growing up in Rockford, Illinois.

But suddenly Jack was interested in prep school, partly because that's what some of his best friends were doing, but mostly because Jack believed he would probably get a better education at a prep school in the East. Jack chose Hotchkiss—totally his choice—because he felt a more structured environment would be better for him at that stage of his life. He figured that out for himself.

Sue and I hated the idea of Jack going away to Hotchkiss. Hated it. But we weren't going to stand in the way of his logical and well-thought-out decision.

I will never forget leaving our boy, fourteen years old, at his Hotchkiss dormitory in some far corner of Connecticut.

That day there was a hole in my heart. And a huge hole in Sue's heart too.

If possible, it got worse once we were back in Florida. For weeks, I could not walk by Jack's room without feeling hurt, and loss, and sorrow.

But I felt he'd made the right choice.

After Hotchkiss, Jack was accepted at Penn, Williams, Vanderbilt, and Brown. He chose

Brown and he loved the school, made dozens of great friends, and never got a B during his four years.

I always told Jack that I wasn't *proud* of him—I was *happy* for him. What I meant was that he had made his own choice—not my choice or Sue's choice—and we were happy that he was doing so well and doing what he needed to do for himself.

You go, Jack.

dolly, hello

I'LL TELL YOU one more love story, the most recent one. I fell head over heels in love with Dolly Parton the first time I met her in Nashville.

I had a half-baked but potentially really good idea for a story about a country singer. I suggested to Dolly's manager that she and I consider writing a novel together. Dolly was interested but she wanted to meet—face-to-face—before deciding. We needed to talk, to get to know one another, if we were going to be writing partners. That made perfect sense to me.

So I took a plane ride to Nashville, a city I've loved since I attended Vanderbilt. Her driver picked me up at the airport. You can tell a lot about rich or famous people by talking to the folks who work for them. The driver had been with Dolly for over twenty years. He told me she was the best, the kindest person on the planet. He loved her and said everybody did. I believed him because of the way he said it. Also because Dolly's reputation precedes her.

That day at her very homey office, I found her to be down-to-earth, genuine, thoughtful, smart as a whip, funny, and self-deprecating. Those are qualities that are right up my small-town alley. There's a line that was used to promote the *Friday Night Lights* TV series that I like a lot: "clear eyes, full heart." That's Dolly Parton.

I guess she was okay with me too because we shook on a deal on the spot to write our book. No agents, no lawyers, nothing but a promise between the two of us. That's the way things should work, in my opinion. Get rid of the middlemen.

Dolly's one concern had been that there wouldn't be enough for her to contribute, and she refused to just put her name on the book. I told her that wasn't how this would work. I wanted her help with the outline and then the book itself. She would make our story authentic, because she knows *everything* about the music business. She would make the story strong, because that's what Dolly does best, tell stories. In fact, that's what country music is all about, storytelling.

Plus, there were a dozen or so songs in the novel. I needed a whole lot of help with those. Dolly said, "Jim, I've written thousands of songs. I can write a country song standing on my head. Want to see?"

Two days after I got home, I received an unbelievable surprise. Dolly already had some good ideas about the first draft of our outline. And she'd sent me the lyrics for *seven* original songs. She'd already written seven songs. Can you believe that? Well, it's how it happened.

I still remember sending her pages one Friday night and on *Saturday* getting back this note:

Hey Jimmy James,

Loving it, loving it, loving it!!! Love our red-headed twins and the community guitar at the Nashville roadhouse. Nicely done. No notes on this batch—keep it coming!

Love,
Dolly

Sue wants me to frame the damn note. She can't stop talking about "*Dolly's* novel."

Dolly and I became friends during our collaboration on *Run, Rose, Run*. She calls me "Jimmy James" or "JJ." For her birthday, I sent her one of those silver cups people give to a mom after she's had a baby. I had it inscribed HAPPY BIRTHDAY, BABY.

For my birthday, Dolly sang "Happy Birthday" to me over the phone. She also sent me a beautiful guitar. She inscribed it TO JIMMY JAMES, I WILL ALWAYS LOVE YOU.

How cool is that?

i'm not sure if any of this

really happened

the country-club set

WHEN I WAS growing up, the Powelton Club was the fancy-pants-wear-a-striped-tie-to-dinner country club in Newburgh. The Patterson family didn't belong. Not even close. We didn't have the money, we didn't have the right résumé, and I guess we didn't much care about status. I still don't.

As a kid, I was occasionally invited to swim in the Powelton Club pool. I thought it was pretty enough, with a really high diving board, but kind of overrated if all you wanted to do was cool off on a hot, muggy summer day. Just another swimming hole, only reeking of chlorine. Lots of frolicking kids with big smiles, cowlicks or ponytails, and heavy-looking braces straightening out their teeth.

I wasn't a golf caddie at the club but a friend of mine, Tommy Hefferon, was. When we were in ninth grade, a professional golfer, Tommy Bolt, came to the club to play an exhibition round. My friend worked a deal so that he and I caddied for Bolt and his foursome.

"Thunder" Bolt was infamous on the PGA tour for having a hot temper. He was also called "Terrible-Tempered Tommy." But he was a very good golfer who won the 1958 U.S. Open and was inducted into the Golf Hall of Fame.

That afternoon at the Powelton Club, I was nervous. I didn't play golf. I didn't even know the rules of golf. The front nine went okay without any memorably embarrassing incidents. Then we got to the tenth hole, yet another tight driving hole at Powelton.

As I remember it, Terrible Tommy pushed his drive to the right. It landed in some high grass and weeds. Shouldn't have been a problem. Except that when my friend and I got out there, we couldn't find Terrible Tommy's ball. That almost didn't seem possible. But we looked everywhere, looked again, and there was no golf ball to be found.

Tommy Bolt went bird shit. Then he went bat shit. He was cursing us out. "You little...how could you lose my ball...in those bushes...in that grass?"

Tommy had a point. I didn't know how we lost the ball either. My caddie buddy and I were mystified. The ball must have hit a rock and sailed God only knew where, and He wasn't inclined to help out Terrible Tommy.

Somehow, we finished the round with Bolt and the well-heeled amateurs in his foursome. We got a minuscule tip to split between us. Then my friend and I walked along the rough of the golf course, heading home.

Suddenly my friend started laughing. He reached deep into a pants pocket, pulled out a ball, and said, "Got Tommy Bolt's ball." He'd plucked the pro's golf ball out of the weeds. It didn't seem that funny to me at the time—but what a great line. Tommy Hefferon had stolen Bolt's golf ball out of the low grass.

In retrospect, it was hilarious. *Got Tommy Bolt's ball!*

Occasionally, I play the Powelton Club these days with pals Mike Smith, Bob Hatfield, and Tommy Hefferon. The personnel at the Powelton are always very nice to us. I usually sign a few autographs and I always have a laugh when we play the tenth hole. It's still tight. But I haven't lost a ball there yet.

born to be wild

HERE'S AN OLDIE but a goodie—and definitely a stranger-than-fiction true story.

The Orange County Fair happened once a year, always in July. It's New York State's oldest fair, and I believe it's still an annual event. Back in the 1960s, it was a big deal that drew tens of thousands of visitors in cars and school buses and church vans that filled several fairground parking lots.

The summer I was eighteen, I was walking through one of the lots on a beautiful sunny day, blue skies, puffy clouds, all that good stuff. I spotted a car that I loved at first sight. A two-tone Pontiac GTO convertible, powder blue and white.

I couldn't believe what I saw next—the keys were in it.

I have no idea what I was thinking, probably

because I wasn't thinking, but I opened the door and got into the Pontiac. I scrunched down low in the driver's seat. I loved the car even more once I was nestled inside. It still had that irresistible new-car smell.

I turned on the ignition. Paused for a couple of seconds. Thought about it. Revved the engine. Then I took off out of the Orange County fairgrounds.

This was my car now. I'd "borrowed" that beautiful, sweet-smelling, dangerously fast convertible. A classic joy ride was now in progress.

I was scared but I was also riding on the outer edge of either heaven or hell. I was old-lady careful at first, then I got onto 9W and opened the GTO up. I flicked on the radio and listened to some rock 'n' roll. Chuck Berry's "Sweet Little Sixteen" was one of the songs. Not quite Berry's "Maybellene" but pretty damn good.

I finally partially regained my sanity and brought the Pontiac back to the fairgrounds. As far as I could tell, nobody was out in the lot searching for their missing car. No harm, no foul. But if I had gotten caught on that perfect summer day—big foul, big harm. I might not be writing this book right now.

On the other hand, maybe I would have

served time in juvie, then gone on to win the Nobel Prize in Literature. Or at least an Academy Award. Hollywood loves its outlaws.

I don't think I've ever confessed about the joy ride. So this is a first. The crazy thing is, to this day, I don't know why I did such a dumb thing. Maybe I needed to be a bad boy for an afternoon. If you're young and stupid and reading this, keep being young, but don't be stupid.

And, yeah, it really happened.

I can still see that two-tone convertible in my mind's eye. I can almost smell that new-car leather.

i'm afraid you have
terminal cancer

the grim reaper—we've met a couple of times, once at my birth

I'VE ALWAYS BEEN pretty good at accepting what life throws at me, whether it's not being able to walk or run the way I used to or eat what I want to eat or remember people's names and on and on, until death shuts me up. I even have an idea for a couple of life-and-death T-shirts. ONE MINUTE YOU'RE HERE . . . THE NEXT, YOU'RE NOWHERE. Or: ONE MORNING YOU JUST DON'T WAKE UP. LIVE WITH IT.

A few years back, I had prostate surgery at the Mayo Clinic. Basically, it sucked. Not the Mayo Clinic; those folks were great. Especially Angela Hoot, who took me to my tests and appointments and whose wonderful name I used for the main character in my novel *1st Case*.

The recuperation from surgery mostly sucked too. But if I hadn't been tested, I might not be writing now. No more James Patterson, no more Alex Cross—and, for me, no more hot fudge sundaes (once a month).

So anybody who is listening to or reading this, if you're a male of a certain age, talk to your doctor about whether you should get tested. If you have a *loved* male of a certain age in your life, or even a *liked* one, tell him to talk to his doctor about getting tested.

If you want to kill some guy, or at least have him neutered, advise him *not* to talk to his doctor about getting tested. There's an idea for a nasty mystery novel.

A year or so after the prostate incident, a small spot was found on one of my lungs. Turned out, it was cancer. So we had to get rid of the spot. Out, out, and all that. This time, I'd be visiting New York–Presbyterian. The same talented surgeon who'd operated on Ruth Bader Ginsburg worked on my lung. I'm fine now. Not even considered at risk. My regular doc, Bruce Moskowitz, calls me "the poster boy for preventive surgery." That works for me.

Soon after the lung operation, I was on the road with President Clinton. He's had a couple of heart operations and told me he'd read that for every hour a patient is under anesthesia, it could take two weeks for the brain to fully recover. There might be some truth in that.

For five or six weeks after the operation on my lung, my imagination wasn't working so well. I was present, but I *wasn't* present. That occasionally clever little voice in my head that usually asks, *What about this? What about that?*—there was no voice. I was no longer mildly schizophrenic.

I wasn't liking it. It was a bit frightening and, honestly, kind of sad. I was lonely without the voice in my head. But I accepted it.

Then, slowly, my imagination came back. Now I think it's working pretty well. Look at all the stories I've made up in this book.

My semi-comforting fantasy about death goes like this: Whatever came before my time on Earth seems to have been relatively peaceful—as far as I know, anyway—so I'm hoping that whatever follows will be equally peaceful.

I've found that the scarier things get, the more humorous I tend to be.

I'm sure it's a defense mechanism, but it's useful. I'm decent at public speaking—because I'm scared shitless when I'm up on that stage. So I get funny. Consider this for a second or two: We all live in a murder mystery, right? We're definitely going to die. *I am, therefore I will die.* We just don't know when, we don't know how, we don't know where.

I once told a writer at *Vanity Fair* that I'd like my obituary to begin like this: "He was slowing down at a hundred and one and had only finished four novels that year."

I'm okay with those numbers.

Until I'm a hundred and one.

$5,000-a-plate dinner stories

$5,000 a plate to listen to me? seriously?

ONE TIME, AND this is off-the-wall nuts, I was offered a cool half million dollars plus a round-trip private-jet ride to give two speeches over two days in Abu Dhabi. It turned out to be a hustle but it was a good one. Fooled one of the top speakers' bureaus.

Up to then, my highest speaking fee had been seventy-five thousand, which is absurd. Actually, it happened *twice*—which is doubly absurd. Both times in Las Vegas. So suddenly it makes some sense, right? (What happens in Vegas and all that.) Both appearances included an armed bodyguard. I guess that would be bad for Vegas's image—"James Patterson Gunned Down at the Bellagio!" Or maybe it would be good for Vegas? Look what Bugsy Siegel did for the town.

I've also been honored to give ten college-commencement speeches, the tenth being at my wife's alma mater, Wisconsin. The Wisconsin speech was filmed in our kitchen and went out online because of the pandemic. The last thing I told the graduates was "Remember this: Nobody will ever forget the class of 2020! Go, Badgers!" Sue gave the speech an A minus. High praise indeed. Even her cousins the Ormsons gave me a passing grade.

I've spoken at $1,000-a-plate charity balls. And one $5,000-a-plate dinner. I'm not even going to comment on that.

Mostly, I choose to give pro bono speeches to kids or large groups of teachers or librarians. I like the enthusiasm of the audiences. For one thing, they're readers. Interestingly, librarians are particularly lively—those crazy little book addicts get all my jokes and most of my obscure literary references.

After I'm introduced, I sometimes start with the line "Hi, I'm Stephen King." That gets a big laugh, since a lot of folks know that Stevie and I aren't exactly tight. His loss. My loss. Our loss. The reason I start with a joke is that I think it's important that the audience know it's okay to laugh, that I don't take myself that seriously and neither should they.

I suspect you know that by now.

i was a tv star for a minute and a half

I LIKE TO start fundraising dinners with this story about my short-lived career as an actor.

I was on the TV show *Castle* a couple of times. *Castle* was a mystery-comedy about a crime writer who partners with a beautiful NYPD detective. Just like in real life, right?

In my two appearances, I was part of a high-stakes poker game the show's hero, Castle, threw with real-life writers Michael Connelly, the late Stephen Cannell, and myself.

Okay, so now it's a couple of years later. My acting career is a memory. I'm minding my own business, strolling down the aisle on a flight from south Florida to New York.

A woman starts jabbing a bejeweled finger at me from her seat in first class. She's clearly very excited and she starts saying, *"I know you! I know you."*

So I stop to talk to her and calm her down. Who knows; maybe she's a distant cousin? Or maybe she's pointing at somebody walking behind me?

I'm kind of used to this routine by now. People will come up to me in restaurants—often as I'm guiding a trembling spoonful of chicken noodle soup to my mouth—and they almost always say, "I'm so sorry to interrupt you." But they do it anyway. That's cool. Why cry over spilled chicken noodle soup?

So the lady on the plane gets out one more "I know you." Then she delivers a great line: "You played Patterson on *Castle*."

I laughed out loud. And I'm still telling the story.

i end a lot of speeches with this story

I LOVE THIS next story because it resonates with just about everybody.

The *San Francisco Chronicle* carried a front-page article about a female humpback whale who had gotten herself tangled in a web of fishing lines and crab traps about twenty-six miles from the Golden Gate Bridge.

The whale was trying to pull hundreds of pounds of traps and ropes out to sea. It was clear she was going to die soon.

A rescue team arrived. The prognosis was as obvious as it was heartbreaking. There was talk of putting the whale down.

Finally, it was decided the only way to save the whale was for all of the rescuers to get in the water and try to untangle the whale by hand. This was definitely a Hail Mary.

The response team worked for half a day

using curved knives and their bare hands. News helicopters began to show up and circle overhead. Finally, close to nightfall, the volunteers worked a miracle. They beat all of the impossible odds.

They had freed the whale.

What happened next surprised and shocked every one of these very wet and tired men and women. A second miracle took place.

When she was free, the whale didn't rush out to sea. Instead, she swam around and around her rescuers in joyous circles. The whale came up to each and every diver one at a time. She nudged them, pushed them gently—maybe as her way of thanking them. What else could it have been?

Several of the rescuers wept and later said it was the most incredibly beautiful moment of their lives.

They said they would never be the same after the experience.

And that is the best story I've ever heard to explain how it feels when you do a good deed and help somebody. *You'll never be the same after the experience.*

the five balls

I FIRST HEARD this touching parable when I was working at J. Walter. It might have helped me find my way out of advertising hell. Maybe that's why I've included it in nearly every one of my college-graduation speeches. Graduates and especially their parents come up to me afterward and say it was their favorite...

Imagine life as a game in which you're juggling five balls in the air.

Let's name them work, family, health, friends, and spirit. Somehow you're keeping all those balls in the air. That's not an easy thing to do.

Sound familiar? Sound a little like your life? Well, it definitely sounds like mine.

Hopefully, you come to understand that work is a rubber ball. If you drop it, it will usually bounce back.

But the other four balls—family, health, friends, and spirit—are made of glass.

If you drop one of these, it will be irrevocably *scuffed, marked, nicked, damaged,* or even *shattered.* It will never be the same.

Once you understand that, maybe, just maybe, you'll strive for more balance in your life.

A related story just popped into my head.

I was scheduled to appear on a morning television show to promote my novel *The Lake House.* Being a guest on morning TV is a big deal for a writer. Little, Brown had given the network an exclusive, which is usually the way it works.

Very late the night before, I got a phone call from Anne Denyeau, the wife of my friend Joe. He had been very sick with cancer. Now Anne told me Joe might not make it through the next day. He wanted to see me. Could I come to their house in New Jersey the next morning?

I called the PR person at Little, Brown and told her I had to back out of the TV appearance. I told her why. She understood, though she wasn't happy about having to break the news to the booker at NBC. I didn't blame her, and honestly, I wondered if I was making the right decision.

Early in the morning, my buddy Ned Mahoney and I took the trip from Westchester to Ridgewood, New Jersey, to see our friend.

Joe's family was gathered in the living room of their house. Joe was in a bed they'd set up on one side of the room. Unfortunately, he hadn't opened his eyes or spoken for several hours. Anne apologized for getting Ned and me to make the trip.

The two of us sat down beside Joe's bed. We said a prayer or two. Then I had a crazy idea. Joe was infamous for arriving late to every imaginable event, but especially tee times for our monthly golf games.

I leaned in close to him and spoke. "Joe! Where the hell are you? You're late. We're on the first tee!"

Joe's eyes popped open. He saw who was there—Ned Mahoney and me. He smiled. Then Joseph went back to sleep.

But you know what? I didn't drop one of those glass balls that day. Ned Mahoney and I were right there where we needed to be—with our friend.

a drive-by book signing or two

HERE'S ONE OF my favorite bookstore stories. It happened to me in New York City.

Sometimes I'll stop by a store, occasionally unannounced, and just sign some books. It's a little bit of an ego trip, but mostly I do it because I love being in bookstores.

(A related, funny story. The mystery writer Lawrence Block—he wrote *Eight Million Ways to Die* and *A Walk Among the Tombstones*—used to sign so many of his own books that collectors said the only valuable Larry Block book was one he hadn't signed yet.)

Anyway, I did this drive-by signing at a large indie bookstore in downtown Manhattan. The staff was pumped up that I came to visit. Big toothy smiles. Damp handshakes all around.

We were all practically dancing in the aisles, slapping high fives, hooting and hollering.

Well, *I* was hooting and hollering. Bookstores still make me feel a little giddy, a little high. I remain a book junkie and I'm proud of it. I can still remember buying novels for a quarter or as much as a buck back in Cambridge, Mass.

The owner told me he had a couple hundred of my books ready to be signed, all turned to the title page, just the way collectors like it.

Sure enough, the books were neatly laid out on a long table at the rear of the store.

Two hundred *Richard North Patterson novels.*

So I signed them.

At another store I stopped at for an impromptu signing, the manager told me she loved my books. She said she'd read all of my Alex Delaware novels. I told her I was a fan of *Jonathan Kellerman's* Alex Delaware novels myself.

That should get a smile out of Kellerman anyway.

finally, some good writing in this book

SPEAKING OF JONATHAN KELLERMAN, there are some really fine writers out there. Several have influenced my work for the better. I like to give them airtime when I speak in public. I'll do the same now. Here's what writers have to say about the "glories" of the writing life.

The sportswriter Red Smith observed, "Writing is easy. You just open a vein and bleed."

This on-target advice came from an Army Ranger scribbler: "If you're ever an Army Ranger in a Black Hawk helicopter, about to land in the dead of night and capture the next Osama bin Laden—here's what you do: legs in, butt tight, mind blank, goggles down, bolts checked, straps pulled and tested, grenades and flares at the ready, relationship to God figured out."

Dorothy Parker offered this characteristically

witty advice to anyone who knows some poor wannabe writer: "If you have any young friends who aspire to become writers, the second greatest favor you can do them is to present them with copies of *The Elements of Style*. The first greatest, of course, is to shoot them now, while they're happy."

Paul Theroux shared this about author moms: "Notice how many Olympic athletes effusively thanked their mothers for their success? *'She drove me to my practice at four in the morning,'* etc. Writing is not figure skating or skiing. Your mother will not make you a writer. My advice to any young person who wants to write is: leave home."

Woody Allen came up with this: "Lay your proboscis on the grindstone. Don't look up. Work. Enjoy the work. If you don't enjoy the work, change occupations."

And finally, from the novelist Richard Ford: "Marry somebody you love and who thinks you being a writer's a good idea."

I took Richard Ford's advice.

gotcha, james!

SOMETIMES I'LL AGREE to a question-and-answer session before a live audience, and the moderator will pull a trick to keep me on my toes, properly focused, and in my place as a humble scribe.

One night in Atlanta, I was asked these ten questions, rapid-fire:

"James, what's your absolute favorite word? This will tell us a lot about you."

"Favorite word? *Yes.*"

"*Yes?* Really? What's your least favorite word? *No?*"

"Actually, it's *elitist.*"

"You're decisive, anyway. What turns you on creatively or spiritually or emotionally?"

"Open minds. On all three counts—creative, spiritual, and emotional."

"And, if I might ask, what turns you off?"

"You may ask. Kind of obvious, though.

Closed minds. There's a lot of that going around these days."

"Not on this stage. Okay, what is your favorite curse word?"

"*Shucks.* Which, to be honest, is total bullshit."

"Love honesty. What sound or noise do you love?"

"*Ka-ching.*"

Not really, but it seemed funny at the time and got a laugh.

"What sound or noise do you hate?"

"*Boo.*"

The audience applauded for that one. Might have been funnier if they'd booed.

"This will tell us something about your character. What profession other than your own would you like to attempt?"

"Nobel Prize–winning author. Why not? It worked out for Bob Dylan."

"Personally, I adore Dylan. And Dylan Thomas as well. What profession would you not like to do?"

"Elevator operator. Toll taker. President of the United States. Any job with *emeritus* in the title. Fish-market employee. It's a tie. Now leave me alone."

"Leave you alone? Clearly, you're unable to

count to ten, James. All right, then, here's your tenth question. If heaven exists, what would you like to hear God say when you arrive?"

"'Great to see you, Jim. Been waiting for this day a long time. We tee off in ten minutes.'"

been around the block a few times

I'VE BEEN POOR and middle class, then poor and middle class again, and now I'm pretty well-to-do. Okay, I'm kind of rich.

On balance, I prefer rich.

But I don't think I would be the person I am, or the writer, if I hadn't experienced the whole spectrum—all the ups and downs and sideways.

We live in crazy times; 2020 and 2021 will probably go down as the worst years in a lot of our lives.

But here's the thing about the problems we're facing—as I see it, anyway.

The problem isn't rich people, or poor.

It isn't men, and it isn't women.

It isn't white, Black, or brown.

Or Republican, Democrat, or Independent.

From what I've seen, the problem is folks

who believe their view of the world is the right one, the only one, and everybody else's is flat-out stupid.

In my mind, the cause of the problems we're facing is pretty clear—it's *jerks.*

I could be wrong. I might just be one of the jerks.

take some chutzpah, add a pinch of hubris

SO, IN THE end, here's what happened to me. I went from a little boy telling stories to entertain himself as he wandered through the woods to a shy kid making a transition from an upstater to a New Yorker to a bestselling writer with enough confidence, or maybe hubris, to speak in front of crowds as large as sixty thousand or smaller crowds paying as much as $5,000 a plate for a rubber-chicken dinner and me.

I just kept telling stories.

Like this one. So simple. But a favorite of mine.

Joyce Hall, founder of Hallmark greeting cards, was a leader, a good employer, and beloved in the Kansas City area, where Hallmark has its headquarters.

When Joyce Hall died in his sleep at age

ninety-one, the *Kansas City Star* ran a front-page banner headline: "Dear God, We Cared Enough to Send You Our Very Best."

There's a good story—*in an epitaph*. I've noticed that a lot of people wear their philosophies, *their life stories,* on their T-shirts, their fishing hats, their license plates, their biceps. One that I've seen in Florida goes LIFE BEGINS WHEN THE CHILDREN LEAVE HOME AND THE DOG DIES.

A couple of months before the virus hit New York, I saw a Wall Street messenger wearing a T-shirt that read THERE'S ALWAYS ROOM FOR IMPROVEMENT AND THEN YOU DIE.

Good one, bike guy.

Stories can even elect presidents.

During the 1992 primary, Bill Clinton's story was seen by detractors this way: a slick, Southern yuppie, educated in silver-spoon schools like Yale and Oxford, a draft dodger who had smoked pot and cheated. Not a good story.

An opinion-research program called the Manhattan Project uncovered a story that changed a lot of minds. The story was this: Bill Clinton was a son of a single mother, a middle-class guy who worked his way up to the Arkansas governorship, where he made remarkable progress in his poor state, focusing on job creation and education.

Now, that's a good story. It helped elect a president.

Here's one of my favorite $1,000-a-plate-dinner stories.

A classically trained pianist and violinist named Emily Zamourka had been homeless for two years or so in Los Angeles after the street performer's $10,000 violin was stolen. One evening, she took the wrong train. Emily got off at the almost empty Wilshire/Normandie LA Metro station. She cursed herself a little, then plopped down on a bench.

As she waited for another train, she thought, *Oh, I'm gonna sing a little bit, maybe that'll make me feel better.*

Emily started to sing a Puccini aria. She was loving it, really belting it out. Then she noticed a police officer walking her way.

She got nervous. Was she creating a disturbance? Would she get a fine that she couldn't afford to pay?

But the LAPD officer just asked whether he could film her on his phone while she sang.

That night he posted the video along with this note: "Four million people call LA home.

Four million stories. Four million voices...
sometimes you just have to stop and listen to
one, to hear something beautiful."

I couldn't agree more.

A few years back, my sister Mary Ellen lured
me over to her side of Florida to give a speech
for a local charity.

She decided to introduce me herself. She was
wearing a big grin as she stood at the microphone. Mary Ellen is such an evil little witch.
"Here's all you have to know to put Jim in
proper perspective—my brother is a jerk!"

Well, Mary Ellen brought the house down
with that one. She was a hard act to follow.
Just like when we were kids.

hey, i'm writing here

THE OTHER DAY I was catching a quick lunch at the Surf Side Diner in town. Actually, the Surf Side isn't that close to the surf. Anyway, I'm alone. Making some notes for a novel I'm doing called *Lion & Lamb*. I'm having a fine time. Doing what I love.

A man I've never seen before comes up and stands over my table.

He finally says, "No friends?"

I look up from my writing. I smile. "Oh, when you're schizophrenic like me, you're never completely alone."

The man I've never seen before shakes his head. "I don't follow. Actually, I'm thinking about writing a book myself. I know who you are. Got some advice?"

"This might sound a little dumb, but go write the book."

"Yeah, that does sound dumb."

He walks away.

I go back to my clam chowder and *Lion & Lamb*.

Whenever I speak in public, I usually say something like this: "Please, please don't send me your manuscript or outline or even your book's riveting first chapter. And I do hope that it's riveting. I really do. I'm rooting for you."

I'm not trying to be unsympathetic or, in the words of my sister Mary Ellen, *a jerk*. Try to look at it this way. Imagine that you vaguely know a local doctor. You see the doctor walking down the street. You approach. Your pace quickens. You social-distance and say, "Hey, doc who I don't really know that well, can you take a look at my X-rays? Tell me what you think."

That's what it's like. Strangers send me manuscripts in the mail or hand me their unpublished books on the street or come up to me in the middle of lunch. People have left seven-hundred-page first drafts in my driveway and on the front steps of my house. They don't stop to think that it takes several hours to read a manuscript, and in the end, unfortunately, it might not be a good result for either of us.

The last thing in the world I want is to have to tell somebody, "Gee, nice try." Or "What do I know, but I had some trouble getting into your thousand-page book."

Sometimes it's worse. If I read a manuscript and say, trying to be nice, "There's some good things about your story," a rewrite of the manuscript will eventually appear on my doorstep. Now I have to spend another six or seven hours reading the rewrite.

I have actually been accused of "skimming" in my rereading of a total stranger's rewrite. And to tell the truth, I did skim a little.

It's especially hard to turn people down face-to-face. Recently, another stranger came up and asked me to cowrite his autobiography. I wanted to be polite, but I couldn't hold back a smile. I asked the man, "How can I cowrite your *autobiography?*"

He said—I swear this is true—"You're the writer, not me."

and now, a word
from flaubert

how it feels to be a writer

I COULD BE wrong, but I think I remember from my grad-school days at Vanderbilt that Gustave Flaubert wrote up to eighteen hours a day, including several letters to the poet Louise Colet. Some scholars believe that the correspondence helped to spark Flaubert's masterpiece *Madame Bovary*. I don't know about that—I never actually got to chat with Gustave Flaubert—but something he wrote in the letters captures the way I feel whenever I sit down to write.

And since I write 350 to 360 days a year, I feel this way pretty much every day.

Flaubert wrote: "It is a delicious thing to write, to be no longer yourself but to move in an entire universe of your own creating. Today, for instance, as man and woman, both lover and mistress, I rode in a forest on an autumn afternoon under the yellow leaves, and I was also the horses, the wind, the words my people uttered, even the red sun that made them almost close their love-drowned eyes."

Yeah, that's what it's like to write and it's why I am such a lucky, lucky person. I get to tell stories every day. This time, the stories of my life.

Like a lot of things in this crazy world, I find it more than a little funny, and also a little sad, that I'm the bestselling writer in the world. I'm okay with it, though. Who in their wrong mind wouldn't be?

THE END

oh no ... there are *more* stories *after* the end

if you're skimming the book looking for your name, it might be here

HEY, YOU GOTTA have friends. My close friends are the best, the nicest human beings. They're funny, or at least have a good sense of humor. There isn't a nasty person in the lot. I'm lucky to know them.

This is dangerous because I'll probably leave somebody I really like out, but here goes. My three sisters—Mary Ellen, Terry, Carole—are precious to me. They have my back, and I have theirs. Always. No matter what. Until death or whatever. The same goes for their very cool kids, Brigid, Meredith, and Andrew. Bob Hatfield, Mick Fescoe, Mike Smith, and Tom Hefferon are old friends from our Newburgh days. Hatfield once paid me a great backhanded compliment. He said, "You're still the same asshole you always were." Meaning, I hope, that I haven't changed too much because of…whatever the hell happened to me after I left the Hudson Valley. Frank Nicolo, Mike Hart, Merrill Snyder, Hal Friedman, Peter de Jonge, Linda Kaplan, and Richard DiLallo all somehow survived the blazing fires of advertising hell. Ned Mahoney, Tom McGoey, Jim Dowd, Mike Guadagno, and B. J. Stringer made it with me through the inquisitions of Catholic college. They're all pretty nice grown-ups. Marie Pugatch was a head nurse at McLean Hospital, but she could easily have been a patient. (Just kidding.) Jeanne Galleta was the sweetest high-school crush anyone could ever have—and Jeanne is the model for Rafe Khatchadorian's middle-school girlfriend in the book and movie. Kathy McMahon was a third-degree black belt and my close confidante and dear friend during our time at J. Walter. Lynda Cole was my bud at Vanderbilt and is still a wonderful cross-country pal (even though she sold out and became a lawyer). Nick Zeppos is my other treasured BF from Vanderbilt. Tony Peyser has been charged with keeping our family solvent, which he's accomplished brilliantly and patiently. (I live in a really nice house.) Tony *is* family. Susan Sandon and Dame Gail Rebuck are my favorite people in all of England, probably in all of

Europe. Jim Karp is my favorite person from Louisville other than Muhammad Ali and, oh yeah, Jim's beautiful wife, Irene. John Abate is my golf partner and go-to person about all things sports, especially the Yankees. The same goes for Craig Jackson, except for the part about the Yankees. Then there's Art Marshall, Jack's faithful godfather, and Terry Marshall, Art's faithful wife. Ned Rust is my partner in crime writing and bureaucracy-bending. Ned's the one who actually got this book started, who kept shamelessly pimping me to write it. Go, Ned! Michael Pietsch is the best editor I've ever had. Denise Roy is coming on strong. The great Mario Pulice, totally fabulous art director. Bob Barnett, my lawyer *and* a great friend, which almost doesn't seem possible. Lawyer *and* friend? Deneen Howell—oh God, another lawyer friend, but more important, the brains behind Mr. Barnett. Dennis Abboud is that rare CEO who is smart as hell, fair, and refreshingly down-to-earth. Bill Robinson's a real sweetheart, and very smart, who puts up with me on an almost daily basis. Of course, I put up with Mr. Bill too. Tim Malloy, journalist par excellence, my partner on *Kid Stew* and the Jeffrey Epstein book and documentary.

And Tim's smart, funny, gorgeous bride, Susan. Frank Costantini and Brian Sitts, the really Big Brains behind *Kid Stew*. The great, very talented Tina Flournoy, "president-herder." Lois Cahall, close friend to nearly everyone in the free world, thankfully including me. Okay, who did I forget? Oh yeah, Mike Lupica is growing on me. Nice man, lots of good stories, fine writer—for a Boston College grad. Is that a two-year school?

What about my other cowriters? Hey, they already got their own chapter.

For one of my big birthdays, I invited a dozen close friends plus some family to keep me company and sing the birthday song really loud. We celebrated in a small room above the kitchen of our favorite Italian restaurant, La Sirena in West Palm Beach. Sue, Jack, Mary Ellen, Carole, Terry, and others showed up. There was only one rule: Absolutely no presents for the birthday boy. But when my friends and family got there, I gave each of them a present. And these were really good presents.

Then I stood at the head of the table and told them why they were each special to me, in particular my three darling sisters, my beautiful bride, and our handsome son. It was a nice evening for me and I think for everybody else in the room.

Hey, you ought to enjoy your own birthday party, right? With some family, some friends, and some tasty Brunello.

dog-eared and well-loved books

IF YOU ARE what you read, then this is an essential element of my story. A few years back, I bought about a half a ton of books that were important to me at different stages of my life. I didn't go to Bauman's to purchase pristine first editions for hundreds, even thousands of dollars. I'm not cheap. Well, I'm a little cheap. But I went out and bought used copies. I like books that look and feel like somebody actually read them, and maybe reread them.

My taste in books, and pretty much everything else, is all over the lot. I can prove it right now. Here are some of the books that mean something to me for all sorts of personal reasons.

The Tin Drum, Günter Grass
Mr. Bridge and *Mrs. Bridge,* Evan S.
  Connell Jr.

Setting Free the Bears, John Irving
One Hundred Years of Solitude, Gabriel
  García Márquez
The Exorcist, William Peter Blatty
The Day of the Jackal, Frederick Forsyth
Eye of the Needle, Ken Follett
The Bonfire of the Vanities, Tom Wolfe
The Autobiography of Miss Jane Pittman,
  Ernest J. Gaines
The Book Thief, Markus Zusak
Ninety-Two in the Shade and *The Sporting
  Club,* Thomas McGuane
Night Dogs, Kent Anderson
Double Indemnity, James M. Cain
A Time to Kill, John Grisham
Marathon Man, William Goldman
Anything by Don Winslow or Lee Child
Winter's Bone, Daniel Woodrell
Goodbye, Columbus and *When She Was
  Good,* Philip Roth
A Fan's Notes, Frederick Exley
Push, Sapphire
Matterhorn, Karl Marlantes
Different Seasons, Stephen King
Cogan's Trade and *The Friends of Eddie
  Coyle,* George V. Higgins
Them, Joyce Carol Oates

Gone Girl, Gillian Flynn
The Virgil Flowers novels, John Sandford
The Forever War, Dexter Filkins
The Natural and *The Fixer,* Bernard
  Malamud
Seabiscuit, Laura Hillenbrand
Steps and *The Painted Bird,* Jerzy
  Kosinski
All the Pretty Horses, Cormac McCarthy
The French Lieutenant's Woman, John
  Fowles
The Seven Storey Mountain, Thomas
  Merton
The Color Purple, Alice Walker
Birdy, William Wharton
Red Dragon, Thomas Harris
Play It as It Lays, Joan Didion
Fat City, Leonard Gardner
The Armies of the Night, Norman Mailer
Go Tell It on the Mountain, James
  Baldwin
The Master and Margarita, Mikhail
  Bulgakov
Our Lady of the Flowers and *The Thief's
  Journal,* Jean Genet
City of Night, John Rechy
Dog Soldiers, Robert Stone

Rage, Fear, and *Peril,* Bob Woodward
Anything by Ron Chernow
Nine Horses, Billy Collins
All My Friends Are Going to Be Strangers
    and *Leaving Cheyenne,* Larry McMurtry
How to Live, or A Life of Montaigne in
    One Question and Twenty Attempts at
    an Answer, Sarah Bakewell
The Life and Opinions of Tristram Shandy,
    Gentleman, Laurence Sterne

I could go on, but yeah, I read a lot, and I really like books. All kinds of books.

But especially the ones that are dog-eared, beat-up, and look well loved and well read.

the $0-a-plate lunch

WHENEVER I SPEAK to a large group of librarians or teachers, early in my speech, I'll say, "I'm here to save lives."

I believe that's absolutely true. There are a lot of problems that we can't solve *as individuals:* global warming, water shortages now and in the future, immigration policy, the threat of pandemics. But we do have the power to get our kids reading.

For the last few years, I've been working with the University of Florida. They have a literacy program that flat-out works. It's a damn miracle waiting to happen. It can help teachers become the best that they can be. It will definitely help them teach kids how to read better, faster, and more efficiently. We have the illiteracy vaccine! Now we need a state or two to actually use it.

I visit prisons and I see the same tragic

scene just about everywhere: Young men and young women—too many of them Black and Latinx—in cell after cell. And because they're locked away most of the day, *they read*. Most of them get to be good readers too.

And as I pass those terrifying cells and look in at the sad, angry faces, I think to myself that if they had become readers as kids, a lot of them wouldn't be in prison. And sometimes I think about those who have written so eloquently about the horrors of prison: Nelson Mandela, George Jackson, Oscar Wilde, Ted Conover.

So I desperately want to turn every kid in every classroom into a reading addict. I want to turn them into reading zombies—the Reading Dead.

I want to get every kid in this country reading and loving it. *No child left illiterate.*

Right now, there's nowhere else—not TV, not the movies, not the internet—where kids can meet as many different kinds of people and begin to understand them and maybe learn to accept who they are as they can in books.

In fact, there's nothing kids can do in middle school or high school that's more important than becoming a good reader. If our kids, *your kids*, don't learn to read well, their choices in life will be seriously diminished. That's just a fact. It's science.

If kids don't know how to read, one day there's a good chance they'll get stuck in some job that they hate. And it's not like they're going to be in that job for a couple of months. That job is going to become their life. That's if they can even get a job.

So let's get them reading. Teachers, principals, school boards, give our kids books that are relevant and inspiring and, God forbid, sometimes make them laugh.

Kids should read as if their lives depend on it... because they do.

nan always said, "don't hurt your arm patting yourself on the back"

MY MOTHER WAS a schoolteacher for forty-seven years. Teaching is in my blood. When I think about education and how I can help, it comes down to two questions— *What's in it for the kids? What's in it for the teachers?*

Sue and I *don't* contribute to building funds at schools. We don't want our names plastered on gardens, gates, or library facades. We help get kids reading. We help teachers survive. We help bookstores.

It varies with the year, but we've given as many as 450 college scholarships for kids studying to be teachers. We fund classroom libraries all over the country. How come classroom libraries? Maybe because my mother paid for the books in her classroom and our family couldn't afford it. So I'm painfully aware of the practice, and a whole lot of teachers continue it today.

When we put out the word through our partner Scholastic, over 82,000 teachers asked for help. Wow! In a sad way. That gave us some idea of the need. Recently, we helped 18,000 teachers pay for the books in their classroom libraries.

For years now, Sue and I have given holiday bonuses to folks who work at bookstores. Most people don't understand how little money many bookstore employees make and how incredibly hard they work. We get letters from nearly every holiday-bonus recipient. They're so thankful it's almost embarrassing. The letters say things like "Thank you so much for the bonus. It allowed me to go to the dentist this year." That's a real quote, and it's pretty typical.

So is this one: "This year we're going to buy Christmas presents for my parents for the first time in five years."

God bless the bookstore people.

Okay, and *ow*, my arm really hurts from all those back pats I just gave myself and Sue.

Here's what I hope, though—that you'll give yourself a whole lot of good reasons to pat yourself repeatedly on the back. We need to start rowing together in this big boat of a country. If we don't row together, the boat goes nowhere, or, worse, it just spins around in circles.

i saved the best for last

pop still whispers in my ear

DURING THE SUMMERS in Newburgh, once a week my grandfather would take me on his frozen-food and ice cream delivery route. I was his unsalaried "assistant" and I would have been happy to work for free with Pop every weekday and twice on Sundays.

I was nine or ten and these trips were a special treat for me, a blessed escape from the boredom of home sweet home. Pop and I would be up at four in the morning packing his truck, and before five we'd be on our way. Yahoo! Who could tell what ice cream–delivery adventures were just beyond the Newburgh city limits?

You might think that driving a delivery truck six days a week isn't the most awe-inspiring job in the world.

Not so.

Every morning, my grandfather would head

over the Storm King Mountain toward West Point, and he'd be singing at the top of his voice, his absolutely terrible voice, his singing-in-the-shower-when-nobody's-home voice.

This big, clunky, slightly tippy delivery truck of his would be bouncing all over the road, and he'd sing "Oh! Susanna" or "(Put Another Nickel In) Music, Music, Music" or "She'll Be Coming 'Round the Mountain." Awful songs that were just perfect for his awful voice.

And he told me this. "Jim," he said, "when you grow up, I don't care if you become a truck driver like me, or a famous surgeon, or the president" (stranger things have happened, Pop). "Just remember that when you go over the mountain to work in the morning, *you've got to be singing.*"

And I do.

I hope the same for you.

There's a sign on the desk in my office. It says YOU RETIRE FROM WORK, YOU DON'T RETIRE FROM PLAY.

I think that's enough stories for now.

It's getting late, almost eleven, and I'm still in my office, writing. I guess you're still reading. The roar of the Atlantic and the wind from the northeast is particularly loud tonight. Kind of soothing, though. Jack called from New York earlier, as he does most days. That's pretty cool. We're lucky to have him.

Soon I'll head off to bed, where Sue and I will hold hands until we fall asleep.